W9-AEH-875

NATIONS
OF THE WORLD
BRAZIL

Anita Dalal

RAINTREE
STECK-VAUGHN
PUBLISHERS

A Harcourt Company

Austin   New York
www.steck-vaughn.com

Steck-Vaughn Company

First published 2001 by Raintree Steck-Vaughn Publishers,
an imprint of Steck-Vaughn Company.
Copyright © 2001 Brown Partworks Limited.

Library of Congress Cataloging-in-Publication Data

Dalal, Anita
    Brazil / Anita Dalal.
       p. cm — (Nations of the world).
    Includes bibliographical references and index.
    ISBN 0-7398-1284-X
    1. Brazil--Juvenile literature. [1. Brazil] I. Title. II. Nations of the World (Austin, Tex.)
F2508.5.D35 2001
981--dc21

                                     00–045925

Printed and bound in the United States
1 2 3 4 5 6 7 8 9 0 BNG 05 04 03 02 01 00

Brown Partworks Limited
Project Editors: Robert Anderson, Peter Jones
Designer: Joan Curtis
Cartographers: Colin Woodman and William Le Bihan
Picture Researchers: Brenda Clynch, Lizzie Lachlan
Editorial Assistants: Roland Ellis, Anthony Shaw
Indexer: Kay Ollerenshaw

Raintree Steck-Vaughn
Publishing Director: Walter Kossmann
Art Director: Max Brinkmann

Front cover: Overview of Rio de Janeiro (background); Brazilian woman with basket on head (right); blue parrot (top left)
Title page: Carnival scene in Rio de Janeiro

The acknowledgments on p. 128 form part of this copyright page.

Contents

Foreword

Since ancient times, people have gathered together in communities where they could share and trade resources and strive to build a safe and happy environment. Gradually, as populations grew and societies became more complex, communities expanded to become nations—groups of people who felt sufficiently bound by a common heritage to work together for a shared future.

Land has usually played an important role in defining a nation. People have a natural affection for the landscape in which they grew up. They are proud of its natural beauties—the mountains, rivers, and forests—and of the towns and cities that flourish there. People are proud, too, of their nation's history—the shared struggles and achievements that have shaped the way they live today.

Religion, culture, race, and lifestyle, too, have sometimes played a role in fostering a nation's identity. Often, though, a nation includes people of different races, beliefs, and customs. Many may have come from distant countries. Nations have rarely been fixed, unchanging things, either territorially or racially. Throughout history, borders have changed, often under the pressure of war, and people have migrated across the globe in search of a new life or because they are fleeing from oppression or disaster. The world's nations are still changing today: Some nations are breaking up and new nations are forming.

"Discovered" by the Portuguese in 1500, Brazil had been inhabited by its native people for thousands of years. In the last 500 years, this vast and fertile land of natural wonders has produced a series of booms in timber, coffee, rubber, and gold, which helped fund its economic development. Stretching from the tropical climes of the Caribbean to the temperate south, Brazil has one of the highest levels of biodiversity in the world and is known internationally for the attempts to preserve the rich ecology of the Amazonian rain forest. Modern Brazil is also striving to reduce the huge disparity between rich and poor and to distribute more fairly the substantial fruits of its recent economic growth.

Introduction

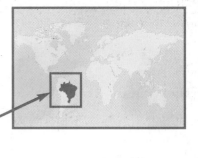

Think of Brazil and what comes to mind? It could be the Carnival in Rio de Janeiro, the mighty Amazon River and its rain forest, or the matchless skill of great Brazilian soccer players such as Pelé and Ronaldo.

Brazil lies in the southern hemisphere and is the largest country in South America. Its area covers 47 percent of South America and 21 percent of the Americas. It is hardly surprising that a country of Brazil's vast size should have a varied landscape. What is remarkable is the extent of the country's diverse plant and animal life. Brazil has one of the richest ecologies of any country in the world.

Unlike most of Latin America, Brazil was colonized not by the Spanish but by the Portuguese. Because of this, Brazilians speak Portuguese, not Spanish. Brazil's history, too, has often been quite different from that of the rest of Latin America. Many Brazilians today are descended from European and African stock and are called *mestiços* (mixed race).

Brazil contains many of Latin America's largest cities. Yet, in the heart of the Amazon rain forest live native South American tribes who have had little or no contact with the outside world. It is the juxtaposition of such extreme opposites that makes Brazil so exciting. However, extremes also blight Brazil. It has the largest disparity in wealth distribution of any country in the world.

The Amazon rain forest covers over one-third of Brazil's land area. In addition there are other large tracts of forest around several rivers in eastern Brazil.

FACT FILE

- Brazil is the largest country in South America, both in terms of area and population.

- Greater São Paulo, with 16.5 million inhabitants, is the world's third-largest city, after Mexico City and Tokyo.

- Rio de Janeiro hosts the largest pre-Lent carnival celebrations in the world. The party lasts for four days.

- Brazil has the largest Japanese population outside Japan. Most live in the center of São Paulo.

- The capital, Brasília, was built from scratch in three years from 1957 to 1960.

The stars on the Brazilian flag represent the 26 states and one federal district. The yellow color represents the country's gold and the green its forests.

LANGUAGE AND PEOPLE

The official name of Brazil is the *República Federativa do Brasil* in Portuguese, or the Federal Republic of Brazil in English. It is shortened to either Brazil (English) or Brasil (Portuguese). When the Portuguese explorer Pedro Alvares Cabral first traveled to Brazil in 1500, he thought the country was an island and called it *A Ilha da Vera Cruz* (Island of the True Cross). When explorers realized they had discovered a country, not an island, they changed the name to *A Terra da Santa Cruz* (Land of the Holy Cross). The country changed name yet again to *Terra do Brasil* (the Land of Brazil Wood) when the Europeans discovered the *pau-brasil* (Brazil tree), which was highly prized because it produced red dye. Until the introduction of sugar cultivation in the mid-16th century, the brazil tree was the country's major commodity.

Currency and Flag

Real bills are colored green for one real; purple for five real; red for ten real, brown for 20; and blue for 100.

Brazil's currency is the real. A hundred centavos make up one real. The real was introduced in 1994, replacing the previous currency, the cruzeiro, in a successful attempt to stamp out the inflation that had dogged the country for much of the late 20th century. Until the introduction of the real, hyperinflation (rapid rises in prices) meant that Brazil was a relatively cheap destination for travelers with a stable currency, such as the dollar. The real is now roughly equivalent to half a dollar.

The Brazilian flag is green with a large golden-yellow diamond in the center. In the middle of the diamond is a blue celestial globe with a white equatorial band, on which is written Brazil's motto: *Ordem e Progresso* (Order and Progress).

Language

The official language of Brazil is Portuguese. Within Brazil, there are regional differences in the way Portuguese is spoken. A native of Rio de Janeiro, for example, known as a *carioca*, has his or her own accent, which a native of São Paulo, known as a *paulistano*, might not understand. *Cariocas* pride themselves on their Portuguese, which is distinctive and is considered to have the accent to emulate. Many other languages are spoken in Brazil because of the country's history of large-scale immigration, particularly Japanese, Arabic, German, English, and Spanish. Before the Portuguese arrived there were probably between three to five million native

Because Brazil has remained as one nation throughout its 500-year history, it has not split into different language groups. Portuguese is spoken by all but the 220,000 native Indians.

The National Anthem

Brazil's lengthy national anthem was composed by Francisco Manuel da Silva (1795–1865). The words are by the poet Joaquim Osório Duque Estrada (1870–1927). The English translation of the first verses is as follows:

The peaceful banks of the Ipiranga
Heard the resounding cry of an heroic
people,
And the dazzling rays of the sun of
Liberty
Bathed our country in their brilliant light.

If with strong arm we have succeeded
In winning a pledge of equality,
In thy bosom, O Liberty,
Our hearts will defy death itself!

O adored Fatherland
Cherished and revered,

All hail! all hail!
Brazil, a dream sublime, vivid ray of love
and hope to earth descends,
Where in your clear, pure, beauteous
skies
The image of the Southern Cross shines
forth.

O country vast by nature,
Fair and strong, brave and colossal,
Thy future mirrors this thy greatness.

O land adored
Above all others,
'Tis thee Brazil,
Beloved Fatherland!

Thou art the gentle mother of the
children of this soil,
Beloved land,
Brazil!

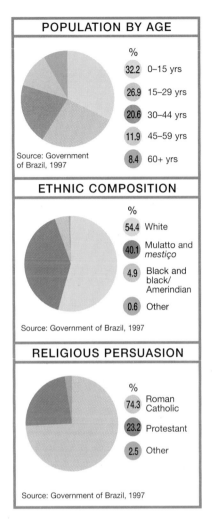

POPULATION BY AGE

%
32.2 0–15 yrs
26.9 15–29 yrs
20.6 30–44 yrs
11.9 45–59 yrs
8.4 60+ yrs

Source: Government of Brazil, 1997

ETHNIC COMPOSITION

%
54.4 White
40.1 Mulatto and mestiço
4.9 Black and black/Amerindian
0.6 Other

Source: Government of Brazil, 1997

RELIGIOUS PERSUASION

%
74.3 Roman Catholic
23.2 Protestant
2.5 Other

Source: Government of Brazil, 1997

The white population of Brazil is descended from European colonialists and settlers. Together with the mestiços—*those of mixed African and European race—they make up the bulk of the population.*

Brazilians. Today, they number around 220,000, split into about 220 tribal groups, each with a unique dialect. Most of the native languages spoken by the tribes belong to four main language groups: Tupí-Guaraní, Ge, Carib, and Arawak.

POPULATION

In 1996, the Brazilian government took a census, reporting the country's population at more than 157 million—although the U.S. Census Bureau records it as higher—making it the fifth-most populated country in the world behind China, India, the United States, and Indonesia. Over the latter half of the 20th century, Brazil changed from a rural society to an urban one. Today, 76 percent of Brazilians live in cities. Greater São Paulo has 16.5 million inhabitants and Greater Rio de Janeiro, more than 10 million. This means that large areas of rural Brazil are sparsely populated. The average population density is 45.8 inhabitants per square mile (17.68 per sq. km), as compared to 64.7 per square mile (25 per sq. km) in the United States. Most of the population is concentrated in the southeast (*see* map opposite).

Brazil's people are young—some 30 percent of the country's population is under 15 years old and only 5 percent is over 65 years old. In 1960, there were 71 million Brazilians. Between the 1950s and 1990s, the

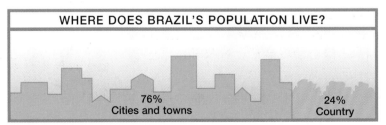

WHERE DOES BRAZIL'S POPULATION LIVE?

76%
Cities and towns

24%
Country

POPULATION DENSITY

Brazil's population is clustered around its eastern coast, where the land is comparatively fertile and where farming has traditionally been possible. There are large built-up areas particularly along the southeastern part of the country. Farther inland, dense forests and high mountains once made much of the land impenetrable to all but the native peoples. As a result, Brazil has both some of the most densely populated and the most sparsely populated areas in the world within its borders.

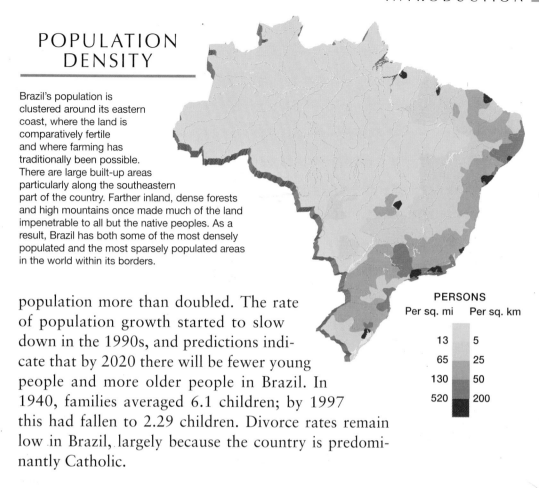

PERSONS

Per sq. mi		Per sq. km
13		5
65		25
130		50
520		200

population more than doubled. The rate of population growth started to slow down in the 1990s, and predictions indicate that by 2020 there will be fewer young people and more older people in Brazil. In 1940, families averaged 6.1 children; by 1997 this had fallen to 2.29 children. Divorce rates remain low in Brazil, largely because the country is predominantly Catholic.

The Plight of Urban Children

Human-rights groups suggest that there are as many as 12 million Brazilian children who do not have either parents or a home. Known as *meninos de rua* ("street kids"), these children live on the streets scratching a living from begging or selling small items such as chewing gum. The fate of these poor children is one of the most pressing human-rights issues facing Brazil. The challenge is to provide essential amenities such as housing, education, and health care that can be used by the whole population.

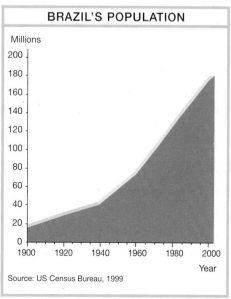

BRAZIL'S POPULATION

Millions

Source: US Census Bureau, 1999

Land and Cities

"Rio is a beauty, but São Paulo is a city."

German-born U.S. film actress Marlene Dietrich

The defining feature of much of Brazil's physical landscape is its sheer scale. Brazil is a huge country. By area, it is the fifth-largest country in the world after Russia, Canada, China, and the United States. At 3,284,426 square miles (8,506,663 sq. km), it is larger than Europe (excluding Russia), and two and a half times the size of India.

Brazil is almost as long as it is wide: 2,684 miles (4,294 km) from north to south, and 2,689 miles (4,302 km) from east to west. From its widest point in the Amazon in the north, the country narrows and tapers toward the south. Brazil shares borders with every other South American country except Ecuador and Chile. Its land borders are shared with Argentina, Bolivia, Colombia, French Guiana, Guyana, Paraguay, Peru, Suriname, Uruguay, and Venezuela. To the east, Brazil has over 4,654 miles (7,491 km) of coastline, stretching from the North Atlantic Ocean to the South Atlantic.

Brazil is a flat country compared with many of its neighbors. The majestic Andes Mountains do not run through the country. Instead, it is dominated by the mighty Amazon River and its huge tributaries. Because most of the country lies south of the equator, the seasons are the reverse of those of North America and Europe: Brazil's summer lasts from December to February and its winter from June to September.

Rio's Sugar Loaf Mountain is typical of the sheer mountains that line Brazil's southeastern coast, crowding buildings into a few miles of available land.

FACT FILE

- Brazil's Amazon tropical rain forest is the largest in the world.

- The Amazon River is the world's largest river in terms of water volume: it contains 20 percent of all the freshwater available on earth.

- Brazil is home to many thousands of unique species of flora and fauna.

- Within Brazil is the wettest place on earth (the Amazon) and one of the driest (the *sertão*).

- At the mouth of the Amazon is the world's largest river island, Marajó, which is only slightly smaller than the whole of Denmark.

BRAZIL'S TERRAIN

Forest
Apart from the vast Amazon rain forest, Brazil has other rain forest regions notably those located around the São Francisco and Araguaia Rivers.

Swamplands
Brazil's most extensive swampland lies in the southwest around the Paraguay River and is known as the Pantanal (*see* p. 23). There are other areas, known as *várzeas*, around the Amazon and Paraguay Rivers which flood regularly and there are small pockets of swampland in the coastal lowlands to the east.

Coastal lowlands
The lowlands along the Atlantic coast are 125 miles in width in the north but at Rio steep cliffs plunge almost directly into the sea. The coastal plain provides the majority of Brazil's farmland.

Highlands
The highlands make up the bulk of Brazil's landmass and are bisected by the country's many rivers. The region is notable for its huge mineral wealth, derived from the vast mountain ranges which once existed here in prehistoric times.

REGIONS AND TERRAIN

Brazil lies mainly south of the equator and stretches south beyond the Tropic of Capricorn. Geographically it divides into four large areas: Amazonia, the Northeast, the Central-West, and the South and Southeast. These regions have differences in both landscape and climate.

The Amazon region is mainly tropical rain forest, but no more than 60 percent of the Amazon rain forest is actually located in Brazil. The rest extends into nine other South American countries. The other three regions of Brazil are each quite different. The Northeast extends into the bulge of Brazil and contains both the *sertão* (dry plains) and the fertile coastal rain forest. In the center of Brazil, south of Amazonia, are large highlands called *Planalto Brasileiro* (Central Plateau). The highlands consist of fertile land used for farming, and the Pantanal, a vast area of wetlands, is home to many unique native species of flora and fauna. The fertile South and Southeast coast contain 60 percent of Brazil's population, although these areas comprise only 18 percent of the country.

~BRAZIL~

VENEZUELA

GUYANA

SURINAME

FRENCH GUIANA

COLOMBIA

Atlantic Ocean

Negro River

Macapá

Equator

Amazon River

Marajó Island

Belém

Amazon River

Manaus

Santarém

São Luís

Fortaleza

Amazon River

Amazonas

AMAZONIA

Tapajós River

Iriri River

Xingu River

Araguaia River

Tocantins R.

Caxias

Paranaíba R.

Teresina

Jaguaribe R.

Natal

Juruá River

Imperatriz

Purus River

Madeira River

Pôrto Velho

Alta Floresta

Tocantins River

Itapicuru R.

São Francisco River

Olinda

Recife

PERU

Rio Branco

CENTRAL PLATEAU

Maceió

Paraguaçu River

Contas R.

Salvador

Cuiabà

BRASÍLIA

Itabuna

BOLIVIA

Goiânia

Minas Gerais

Diamantina

Corumbá

Mato Grosso do Sul

Paranaíba R.

Paraguay R.

Pantanal

Campo Grande

Belo Horizonte

Vitória

Ouro Prêto

Paraná R.

Nova Iguaçu

Petrópolis

Niterói

PARAGUAY

Londrina

Campinas

Paranapanema R.

São Paulo

Santos

Rio de Janeiro

Tropic of Capricorn

Parana

Iguaçu Falls

Iguaçu R.

Curitiba

São Vicente

Paranaguá

Florianópolis

CHILE

Pacific Ocean

ARGENTINA

Jacuí R.

Pôrto Alegre

Pelotas

Rio Grande

Atlantic Ocean

URUGUAY

N

Andes Mountains

KEY

Cities and towns by population

◇ over 5,000,000

▣ 500,000 to 5,000,000

◉ 100,000 to 500,000

● under 100,000

Other symbols

▲ high points

– – country border

15

People of the Rain Forest

In the 20th century, part of the rain forest was cleared to make way for new settlements. Today, about nine million Brazilians live in the Amazon region. A third of these people live in the cities of Manaus, Belém, and Santarém. Many of the inhabitants of Amazonia are poor *caboclos* (villagers). They work as rubber-tappers, brazil-nut gatherers, fishermen, and subsistence farmers harvesting on such a small scale that they do not damage nature. In 1988, Chico Mendes, a rubber-tapper, was murdered by cattle ranchers because he had organized the first local protest to defend the rain forest and its peoples' way of life.

Only 220,000 of the population of Amazonia are native peoples. These comprise tribes, such as the Yanomami, who have lived there for centuries. They survived by harvesting the natural products of the rain forest. They used the naturally poisonous cassava root to make a flour and extracted quinine from the cinchona tree to treat malaria. They gathered wild fruits and berries and hunted and fished. Even today, an estimated 40 tribes exist who have never been contacted by outsiders. The destruction of the rain forest threatens to destroy the native way of life and has brought the plight of Brazil's native peoples to the world's attention.

Amazonia

Covering an area over 2.3 million square miles (6 million sq. km), the Amazon rain forest is the largest tropical rain forest in the world. It is dense, lush tropical forest. The trees grow in different layers. A few kinds of tree, called emergents, grow as high as 150 feet (45 m) and tower above the surrounding forest. Next comes a dense layer of treetops about 80 to 100 feet (25 to 30 m) from the ground. The trees grow so close that they form a canopy blocking out the sun to everything below. At this canopy level, numerous plants thrive, including brightly colored orchids and emerald-green mosses and ferns. Closer to the ground are more canopies of vegetation, made up of saplings (young trees), as well as smaller trees and shrubs. By contrast, the forest floor is mostly infertile and supports little vegetation.

A wealth of wildlife flourishes within this closed environment. Naturalists estimate that the forest is home to 20 percent of the world's plant and bird species, perhaps 10 percent of mammal species, and an immeasurable number of insects. There are as many as 50,000 species of tropical plants and trees, half of which are only to be found in the Amazon region.

The Amazon River has 1,100 tributaries. Seventeen of them are more than 1,000 miles (1,600 km) long.

The thick upper layers and vast length of the trees' trunks lets little light through to ground level.

The Amazon River

The great Amazon River is a record breaker. In terms of the volume of water it carries, the river is the largest in the world, pouring 170 billion gallons of water into the Atlantic Ocean every hour. This is 10 times the volume of the Mississippi River. The volume of water that flows out of the river mouth is so great that freshwater can be found some 200 miles (320 km) out to sea. At its lower reaches, the river is so broad that it is impossible to see from one bank to the other. At 4,000 miles (6,436 km) long, the Amazon is also the second-longest river after the Nile.

The Amazon gets its name from a tribe of women warriors in Greek mythology called the Amazons. The first European to explore the river was the Spaniard Francisco de Orellana. In 1541–1542, he and his men journeyed almost the entire length of the river, traveling from Peru to the river's mouth. On the way, Orellana was attacked by what he thought was a party of female warriors, whom he called Amazons.

The Amazon starts its journey outside Brazil high in the Andes Mountains of Peru, only about 100 miles (160 km) from the Pacific Ocean. At this stage, the river is called the Marañón. As the river flows westward, it collects the waters of over a thousand tributaries, or lesser rivers that do not have mouths on the sea. Important tributaries include the Putumayo (or Içá), Negro, Xingu, and Trombetas.

The tributaries of the Amazon are classified as either black or white. The black water of rivers such as the Negro ("Black") is caused by acid formed from

decomposing material from the forest floor. This water is very pure and contains very few nutrients, which means little animal life can live in black rivers. In contrast, the whitewater rivers are formed by rain and snow run-off from the Andes. They are very rich chemically and full of animal life. Where blackwater and whitewater rivers merge, the color difference is striking (*see right*). At the Amazon port of Manaus, the blackwater Negro runs beside the whitewater Amazon for about four miles (6 km) without mingling.

The Amazon regularly floods. In the upper part of the river, there are two floods every year. This is because the river gathers its water from two distinct climate zones—Ecuador and Peru—where the rainy season falls at different times of the year. Farther downstream, though, there is just one annual flood. The floods are not a disaster but part of the cycle of the seasons. The flooding whitewater rivers create a lowland area of rich soils called the *varzéas*.

Forest is cleared by slashing and burning. Not only are the flora and fauna of the forest destroyed but the burning releases large quantities of harmful gases into the environment.

Everything to do with the Amazon is on such a huge scale that scientists have not yet cataloged half the plants that grow in the rain forest.

Some of the plants that grow in the rain forest are important economically. They yield products such as brazil nuts, rubber, pineapples, and cocoa. Many Amazon trees are prized for their wood, including mahogany, cedar, and rosewood. Some plants are harvested for their medicinal properties. Quinine, cocaine, and curare, for example, all derive from Amazon species and are used in modern drugs. Still others species produce flavorings and perfumes.

Today, the Amazon rain forest is rapidly being destroyed. Loggers cut down millions of trees to supply the timber industry, while farmers clear land to use for grazing cattle and growing crops. During the 1960s, the Brazilian government paid poor farmers from the south of Brazil to settle in the Amazon. It also encouraged industries to move to the area. Between 1970 and 1989, over 150,000 square miles (400,000 sq. km)—roughly 10 percent of the forest—was destroyed. In 1995 alone, an area the size of Maryland was cleared.

The destruction of the rain forest is one of the greatest environmental threats facing the planet. Deforestation is endangering thousands of animal and plant species as well as threatening the way of life of native peoples. And because the rain forest produces one-fifth of the world's oxygen, its destruction also places the survival of the whole earth in jeopardy.

In 1998, the Brazilian government passed environmental laws, with the aim of getting tough on those illegally logging and destroying the forest. Such is the size of the forest, however, and the difficulty of enforcing such laws that the destruction continues today. Photographs taken from the air show the continuing devastation of one of the earth's most precious environments.

The Northeast

The Northeast is the poorest region of Brazil. During colonial times, sugar plantations were set up in the region, making it the country's economic and political center. The main reason for the area's current poverty is its climate. Much of the Northeast lies in a dry, arid area known as the *sertão*, an inhospitable landscape where farming is difficult due to frequent droughts. The soil is stony and the trees and bushes grow twisted, stunted, and covered in thorns. In such a dry landscape many cacti flourish since sometimes it does not rain for as long as a year. From 1979 to 1984, the area suffered the country's worst ever drought.

During the droughts, plants shrivel and seem to die, while farmers and animals go hungry as they await the rain. When the rain arrives, the heavy thunderstorms cause widespread flooding and soil erosion. Despite the harsh conditions, many people live in the *sertão*; in 1990,

Farming in the dry sertão region of the Northeast is hard work and many farmers are dependent on subsidies from the federal government.

The Coastal Region

Brazil's long coastline faces the Atlantic Ocean on one side and the coastal mountain range on the other. The narrowness of the coastal strip has deeply affected the history of Brazil. Until recently, settlers could not penetrate the mountains and so most settlement and economic growth took place on the coastal strip. Today, most of Brazil's major cities lie on or near the coast, where 80 percent of the population live.

Sheer mountains sit right on the coast. Around Rio de Janeiro and Espírito Santo, to the north, the coastal region is rocky and irregular with lots of bays and sudden granite peaks, the most famous of which is the *Pão de Açucar* (Sugar Loaf Mountain) in Rio de Janeiro. North of Bahia the coastal lands flatten out and the transition to the highlands becomes more gradual. Here there are navigable rivers and the coast is calm, protected by offshore reefs. The coast continues all the way to the border with French Guiana.

On the coastal strip grows a rain forest called the Mata Atlântica. It is 60 million years old (20 million years older than the Amazon rain forest). It has been reduced to between 2 and 5 percent of its original size as a result of sugarcane farming, coffee growing, logging, and acid rain. Despite this, it is still rich in wildlife.

there were more than 42 million. However, many others have moved south to the urban centers of São Paulo and Rio de Janeiro to escape the next inevitable drought.

The rest of the Northeast is more fertile, especially the strip which runs south along the coast from the state of Rio Grande do Norte to Brazil's most southerly state of Rio Grande do Sul.

Central-West Brazil

This part of Brazil still has the feel of the Wild West, since it is only in the last 20 years that roads have penetrated the area. Its history is full of adventurers—not least the *bandeirantes* (*see* p. 54) who saw the western states as the last great area to conquer. Much of the area sits on the enormous *Planalto Brasileiro*, or Central Plateau, 3,300 feet (1,000 m) above sea-level with several small mountain ranges and large rivers. The plateau is divided into two areas of forest and woodland savanna known as *cerrado*. Forest is found mainly in the north, and the *cerrado* dominates the plateau. Once cleared, the *cerrado* was found to be extremely fertile and is used for large-scale farming. Reservations of native peoples, the new capital of Brasília, and the great nature reserve of the Pantanal are all to be found in this region.

The Pantanal

The Pantanal is a large natural paradise that is one of the world's last great wildlife refuges. Covering an area of 88,809 square miles (230,000 sq. km), half the size of France, it lies mainly in Brazil but extends into neighboring Bolivia and Paraguay. Although technically not a swamp but a large alluvial plain (an area fed by soils deposited by running water), the Pantanal gets its name from *pantano*, the Portuguese word for swamp.

The seasonally flooded swampland offers the greatest density of tropical wildlife outside Africa. The Pantanal is surrounded by mountains, from which rain flows down, forming the Paraguay River and its tributaries, which flood during the rainy season (December to March). Because it is so flat, most of the area floods; the few roads that cross the landscape become impassable. There are more than 300 species of bird, including the *jabiru*, or giant red-throated stork, 230 types of fish, including the flesh-eating piranha. Birds and animals proliferate due to the lack of people and motor vehicles.

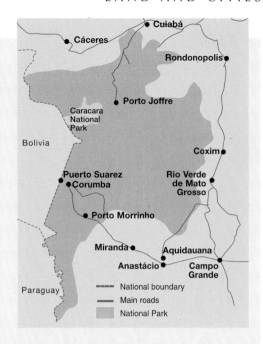

Map legend:
- – – – National boundary
- —— Main roads
- National Park

Caimans are common in the Pantanal, where they crowd together in shallow pools.

The Iguaçu Falls

The Iguaçu Falls lie on the border between Argentina and Brazil and near the border with Paraguay. They are jointly administered by Brazil and Argentina. In Brazil they lie in the southern state of Paraná near the town of Foz do Iguaçu. They are the most spectacular waterfalls in South America and one of the most visited tourist destinations in the southern hemisphere. The falls actually comprise 275 separate cataracts (large waterfalls) which drop a distance of 240 feet (60 m) over a precipice some 1.8 miles (3 km) wide, causing a continuous wall of spray. Above the waters stretch many rainbows. The falls are 65 feet (20 m) higher and half as wide again as North America's Niagara Falls. On both the Brazilian and Argentinian sides the falls are set in large national parks with lush, tropical vegetation and these create a spectacular backdrop to the falling water. Close to the waterfalls is the world's largest dam, the Itaipu, which destroyed the world's largest waterfall, Sete Quedas (Seven Falls), when construction began in the 1970s.

Brazil's National Parks

Brazil has 40 national parks and numerous other conservation areas. The largest are shown on the map on the right. The country enjoys greater biodiversity (diversity of animal and plant species) than any other in the world. Many of these areas are very remote and this makes them difficult to protect from loggers. Environmentalists have therefore argued that the conservation of these areas is as much an international problem as that of the Brazilian government alone, and there have been international campaigns to support local protection plans in Brazil.

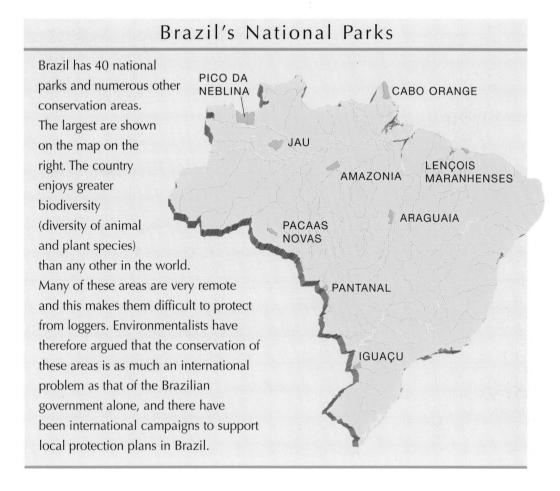

The South and Southeast

These two regions comprise some 18 percent of Brazil's total land area, but hold 60 percent of its population. Brazil's three largest cities, São Paulo, Rio de Janeiro, and Belo Horizonte, are located on the coastal ridge. In the southeast, the landscape beyond the coast comprises rolling hills with an average altitude of 2,300 feet (700 m). Farther south, in the area south of the Tropic of Capricorn, are rolling farmlands where wheat, corn, soybeans, and rice are grown. This prairie region houses many of Brazil's largest farms and cattle ranches. In the eastern half of the state of Rio Grande do Sul, with its mountainous terrain and deep-forested valleys, live Italian and German migrants who established Brazil's wine industry.

THE STATES OF BRAZIL

RORAIMA

AMAPÁ

AMAZONAS

PARÁ

MARANHÃO

CEARÁ

RIO GRANDE DO NORTE

ACRE

PIAUÍ

PARAÍBA

PERNAMBUCO

RONDÔNIA

TOCANTINS

ALAGOAS

BAHIA

SERGIPE

MATO GROSSO

FEDERAL DISTRICT

GOIÁS

MATO GROSSO DO SUL

MINAS GERAIS

ESPÍRITO SANTO

SÃO PAULO

RIO DE JANEIRO

PARANÁ

SANTA CATARINA

RIO GRANDE DO SUL

Brazil is divided into 26 states. In addition, there is one Federal District, the area around the country's capital, Brasília. The states are listed below with their capitals, marked with a dot on the map on the right.

ACRE Rio Branco
ALAGOAS Maceió
AMAPÁ Macapa
AMAZONAS Manaus
BAHIA Salvador
CEARÁ Fortaleza
ESPÍRITO SANTO Vitória
GOIÁS Gioânia
MARANHÃO São Luis
MATO GROSSO Cuiabá
MATO GROSSO DO SUL Campo Grande
MINAS GERAIS Belo Horizonte
PARÁ Belém
PARAÍBA João Pessoa
PARANÁ Curitiba
PERNAMBUCO Recife
PIAUÍ Teresina
RIO DE JANEIRO Rio de Janeiro
RIO GRANDE DO NORTE Natal
RIO GRANDE DO SUL Pôrto Alegre
RONDÔNIA Pôrto Velho
RORAIMA Boa Vista
SANTA CATARINA Florianópolis
SÃO PAULO São Paulo
SERGIPE Aracaju
TOCANTINS Palmas
FEDERAL DISTRICT Brasília

ADMINISTRATIVE DIVISIONS

The states of Brazil encompass widely differing geographical conditions and population levels. For example, the state of Roraima in the northwest of the country has a population of just over 200,000 and an area of 88,843 square miles (230,181 sq. km), while that of São Paulo state, with roughly the same area, tops 31 million. Political power has traditionally originated in the southeastern triangle of São Paulo, Rio de Janeiro, and Minas Gerais, although there is a strong tradition of working-class politics in the northeast.

CLIMATE

Most of Brazil lies in the southern hemisphere. The weather throughout the country varies considerably. The Amazon region receives the most rain in Brazil. The town of Belém receives more than 90 inches (230 cm) of rain a year, making it one of the wettest places on earth. The Amazon is humid year-round but has an average temperature of 80° F (27° C), relatively low for a tropical region. Because Brazil's summer lasts from December to February, celebrating Christmas on the beach is normal for Brazilians.

In the far south of Brazil, the southern states of Rio Grande do Sul, Santa Catarina, Paraná, and São Paulo become quite cold in the winter. In June a temperature of

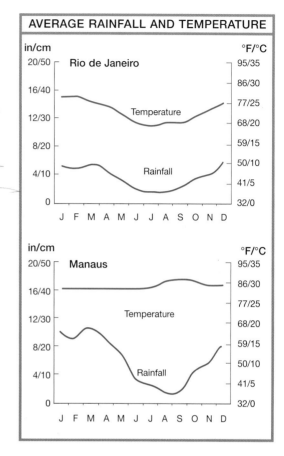

AVERAGE RAINFALL AND TEMPERATURE

Rio de Janeiro

Temperature

Rainfall

Manaus

Temperature

Rainfall

Trade Winds

Since Brazil lies close to the equator, much of its weather is determined by the trade winds. The trade winds blow toward the equator from two directions—the northeast and the southeast. Trading ships once used the winds to propel them across the seas (hence the name). Between December and May the northeast trade wind moves north, resulting in less rain for the Amazon region around Belém and the coastal area around Recife. From the coastal town of Salvador southward, the southeast trades (as they are known) bring in rain from the South Atlantic Ocean. However, the winds never meet. The gap between the two weather systems is known as the "doldrums," the dry area of northeastern Brazil.

Temperatures in the cities of the southeast, such as Rio, are relatively uniform throughout the year. At Manaus, in the heart of the Amazon, intense humidity means that buildings must be constantly repaired and repainted.

55° F (13° C) is not unusual. It even snows in the central highlands of Santa Catarina. Coastal cities such as Rio de Janeiro, however, never get very cold. The temperature in Rio rarely dips below about 70° F (22° C) and at the height of the summer it often exceeds 100° F (40° C) and may reach 110° F (45° C). The rains in Rio come in short bursts and last from October through to April.

The coolest places in Brazil are the highlands (*planalto*) of Minas Gerais and Brasília, where it is invariably cooler than the coast. Wealthy inhabitants of Rio de Janeiro often have summer homes in the hills in towns such as Petrópolis, where they go to escape the intense summer heat.

When it rains across Brazil it is usually in the form of short, intense tropical downpours. The exception is the *sertão*. Once the rain arrives there, it continues to pour down for several months.

Children play in a torrential downpour on Marajó Island, the largest river island on earth, situated on the equator at the mouth of the Amazon.

FLORA AND FAUNA

The Amazon, Pantanal, and coastal regions are a vast ecosystem that has an outstanding number of animal and plant species, many of which are found nowhere else in the world. For botanists and ecologists working in Brazil, so many species have yet to be cataloged and remain unknown that compiling a list of endangered species is almost impossible.

Bromeliads, such as that shown below, are plants that grow on the bark of trees. They take advantage of the light available below the tallest canopies of the forest.

Some species are unique to certain areas of Brazil. The Atlantic rain forest has 17 out of 21 unique primate species (the group that includes apes, monkeys and humans), of which 13 are endangered, including the golden, black lion, and golden-headed lion tamarins. The varied flora of the Atlantic rain forest includes orchids, mosses, lichens, bromeliads, and the monkey-puzzle tree.

The Amazon supports 30 percent of the world's known plant and animal species, among them this brightly colored parrot.

The unique ecosystem of the Amazon region supports 2,000 species of fish, more than 1,800 species of butterfly, and more than 200 species of mosquito. Thousands of birds such as the brightly colored toucan, parrot, and macaw fly beneath the rainforest canopy. In the rivers live the silver-dollar fish, piranha, electric eels, and stingrays, and reptiles such as caiman (a type of reptile closely related to the crocodile) and turtles. Giant otters, manatees, and gray and pink river dolphins swim in the rivers. Boa constrictors live in the rain forest and jaguar, tapir (a hoglike mammal), capivara (which looks like a giant guinea pig), and the armadillo wander the rain-forest floor. The jaguar, caiman, dolphin, and many species of monkey are threatened with extinction largely because of poaching. Scientists worry that many other species have become extinct before they had even been studied.

The Pantanal contains wading birds such as egrets, jabiru storks, spoonbills, and herons, and mammals such as the tapir, marsh deer, and jaguar. The black caiman has been hunted almost to extinction and the marsh deer, the giant river otter, and the jaguar are all threatened.

Brazil is very sensitive to international criticism about the destruction of its rain forest, and since the country hosted the 1992 Earth Summit in Rio de Janeiro (*see* p. 73), it has brought in legislation to protect the environment. There are 40 national parks across Brazil and many other biological and ecological reserves protecting areas of outstanding beauty and unique flora and fauna. They are places of special scientific interest that are also open to the public for recreation and educational purposes.

BRAZIL'S CITIES

Brazil's population is an urban one. Three out of every four Brazilians live in cities and towns, largely for economic reasons. Brazil has some of the world's most densely populated cities. The largest city in population terms is São Paulo, which boasts 16.5 million people, making it the third most populated city in the world (after Tokyo and Mexico City). It is predominantly an industrial center and many people move there from the rest of the country to find work.

Brazil's second most populated city (with ten million inhabitants) is Rio de Janeiro, which until 1960 was the country's political capital. In the 19th century Rio (as it is known) was the city's economic, political, and cultural center. Cities such as Belo Horizonte and Salvador have populations in excess of two million. Brazil's new capital, Brasília, is the least populated of all the country's major cities, with a population of only 1.8 million inhabitants in 1996.

The city of Rio lies on the natural harbor of Guanabara Bay. Rio stretches for over 12 miles (20 km) along the coastal strip.

Rio de Janeiro

Rio de Janeiro is undoubtedly one of the most beautiful cities in the world. The city is long and thin, wedged between the mountains and the Atlantic Ocean. The natives of Rio, known as *cariocas*, have a reputation as happy-go-lucky people who know how to party and have a good time. The best example of *cariocas* enjoying themselves is the pre-Lenten festival of Carnival (*see* p. 101) which lasts for five days.

Because of the narrowness of the available land, most *cariocas* live in tall apartment houses. Lining the side of the hills behind the high-rise buildings that stretch along beaches such as Copacabana and Ipanema are the *favelas* (slums, *see* p. 37). The *favelas* are home to a third of Rio's population. The city's largest *favela* (with more than 150,000 inhabitants) lies in the heart of the wealthy neighborhood of Gávea. Rio is split into two zones, linked by the downtown center: a residential area, the Zona Sul, and an industrial zone, the Zona Norte. The two rarely overlap.

The best way to get your bearings in Rio is to climb above the city. From the top of one of the city's most famous landmarks, the peak called the *Corcovado* (the Hunchback), a spectacular view can be had of the city with the ocean beyond it. The

Central Rio is built around Guanabara Bay. The city's many steep hills mean that areas of crowded buildings are interspersed with unpopulated stretches of vegetation.

RIO DE JANEIRO

The Beaches of Rio

Many of Rio's sights are natural: the beaches, the granite peaks, the botanical garden, and the national parks. The beaches of Rio are one of its most distinctive features. Copacabana is the most famous; it stretches more than two miles (4.5 km) in front of one of the most densely populated residential areas in the world (25,000 people per sq. km).

The sea is too polluted to swim in and at Ipanema Beach a strong undercurrent makes it too dangerous to swim. The beach is more than a place to sunbathe, however. *Cariocas* use it as an outdoor extension to their small apartments. People meet their friends, chat, read, buy things from passing beach vendors, play beach sports such as *footvolei* (a type of volleyball played without using the hands), and generally hang out. The beaches are where the *Cariocas* from wealthier areas rub shoulders with their poorer neighbors from the *favelas*. Crime has been a problem on all the beaches, with the result that they are now heavily policed.

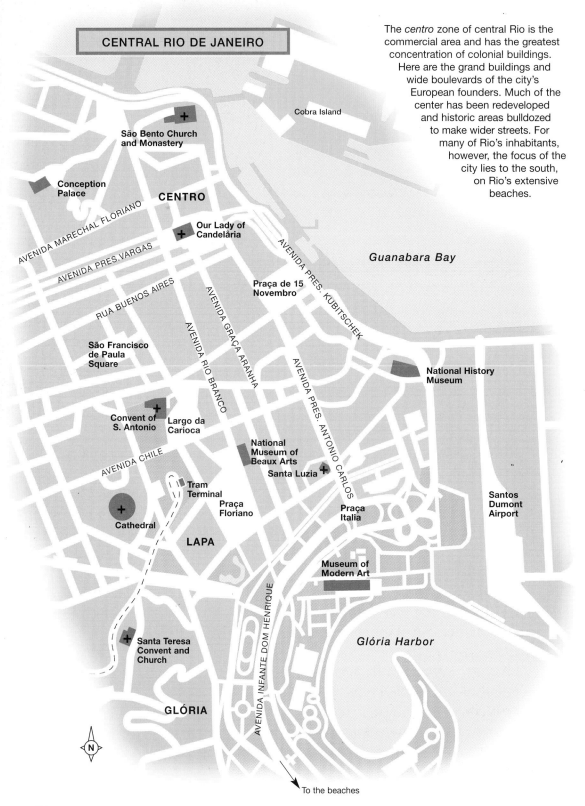

CENTRAL RIO DE JANEIRO

São Bento Church and Monastery

Cobra Island

Conception Palace

CENTRO

Our Lady of Candelária

AVENIDA MARECHAL FLORIANO

AVENIDA PRES. VARGAS

RUA BUENOS AIRES

Praça de 15 Novembro

AVENIDA PRES. KUBITSCHEK

Guanabara Bay

São Francisco de Paula Square

AVENIDA RIO BRANCO

AVENIDA GRAÇA ARANHA

AVENIDA PRES. ANTONIO CARLOS

National History Museum

Convent of S. Antonio

Largo da Carioca

AVENIDA CHILE

National Museum of Beaux Arts

Santa Luzia

Tram Terminal

Praça Floriano

Praça Italia

Santos Dumont Airport

Cathedral

LAPA

Museum of Modern Art

AVENIDA INFANTE DOM HENRIQUE

Glória Harbor

Santa Teresa Convent and Church

GLÓRIA

N

To the beaches

The *centro* zone of central Rio is the commercial area and has the greatest concentration of colonial buildings. Here are the grand buildings and wide boulevards of the city's European founders. Much of the center has been redeveloped and historic areas bulldozed to make wider streets. For many of Rio's inhabitants, however, the focus of the city lies to the south, on Rio's extensive beaches.

Corcovado is almost 2,500 feet high (710 m). Atop the *Corcovado* is a gigantic statue of Christ the Redeemer (*O Cristo Redentor*), which stands some 124 feet high (38 m) at its summit. You can reach the peak either by taking the cog railway, which climbs quite steeply in places, or by road. The last part of the climb (some 220 steps) must be done on foot. If you stand in front of Christ's statue, you will see the Bay of Guanabara straight ahead. Christ's left arm points to the Zona Norte and his right arm to the Zona Sul and Copacabana, Ipanema, and Leblon beaches. Another great view of the city can be seen on a cable-car trip up to the summit of the *Pão de Açucár* (Sugar Loaf Mountain), which is 1,300 feet (396 m) high.

The famous statue of Christ the Redeemer stands on the top of Rio's Corcovado, or Hunchback Mountain. It was completed in 1931 by the French sculptor Paul Landowsky.

Walking Tour of Downtown Rio

The long and narrow layout of the city means that to get from one neighborhood to another you have to travel by car or bus. The subway system in Rio is efficient and reliable but does not extend much beyond the downtown area based around the *centro*.

The center of the city is now the commercial district of Rio, filled with high-rise office buildings. It was the site of the original settlement and is home to colonial buildings that attest to Rio's past. The heart of present-day Rio is the main square, Praça Floriano, which lies to the south of the business district and is located next to Cinelândia subway. It comes to life at lunchtime and after work, when office workers relax over a beer and listen to samba musicians. The Praça Floriano is also the place to hear impromptu political speeches. On the north side of the square is the impressive Teatro Municipal (state theater) which is home to Rio's opera and orchestra. From the theater, walk down the pedestrianized Avenida 13 de Maio and cross the street at Largo de Carioca. Up on the hill is the Convento de Santo Antônio. It is the oldest church in Rio, founded in 1608. Santo Antônio inspires much devotion among local women who make offerings to him in the hope that they will find a husband!

Looking east from the Convento you will see the modern Metropolitan Cathedral with its huge stained-glass windows. These are symbolically colored: green for the clergy, red for the saints, blue for the Virgin Mary, and yellow for the apostles. Beyond the cathedral, and accessible by tram, is the Santa Teresa neighborhood. In the 1800s it was home to Rio's elite who took the *bonde* (tram) downtown to work. During the 1960s and 1970s many artists moved into the area, which had become run down. Today, you can still see many of the old colonial mansions, some of which have been beautifully restored.

The towering Metropolitan Cathedral in Rio was built between 1964 and 1976.

Favelas

Favela is the Portuguese name for the slum housing that springs up on the edge of a city. It originated with 19th-century soldiers who set up camp on a hill called Morro das Favelas (Hill of Nettles) because it was full of nettles (*favelas*). The soldiers became known as *favelados*. When they returned to Rio and built their homes, the nickname stuck and their homes became known as *favelas*. Any temporary settlement then became known as a *favela*. In the case of Rio, they have appeared on the hillsides because of the city's unusual geography. In São Paulo, they are located on the edge of the city.

People move to the shanty towns if they arrive in the city and cannot afford anything better. They hope to move on but often this does not happen. Traditionally, because of the temporary nature of the *favelas'* construction, they are not treated as communities and so lack all basic amenities. Residents tap into electricity and water supplies, often illegally, but basic waste disposal and other facilities such as education and health care do not exist. The shanty towns can be very large—in Rio it is estimated that one million people live in them.

In the 1970s and 1980s some attempts were made to improve the *favela* conditions once it was clear that these temporary homes were here to stay. It was only in the 1990s that a determined effort was made to improve the *favelas*. A program backed by the United States is providing streets instead of alleys and installing sewers, lighting, day-care centers, play areas, trash collection services, and transportation.

São Paulo

The financial and industrial center of Brazil, São Paulo is three times the size of the French capital, Paris. The city has expanded very rapidly since the late-19th-century coffee boom, which made São Paulo state the largest coffee-producing region in the world and attracted many investors from Europe and the United States. In the 20th century the city has boomed again, its suburbs sprawling over an area of 11,580 square miles (30,000 sq. km).

The center of São Paulo is an impressive array of steel-and-glass towers, but away from the center, the slums are no more than wood and cardboard. On the right is the circular tower of the São Paulo Hilton.

Today, São Paulo is a city of skyscrapers, long avenues packed with traffic, and crowds of people. *Paulistanos*, as the inhabitants are known, have a reputation as hard workers and they pride themselves on their work ethic. The main street, Avenida Paulista, is a cross between New York City's Wall Street and London's Oxford Street (a main shopping street). It is home to many multinational companies and designer shops. São Paulo is ethnically

CENTRAL SÃO PAULO

To the airport

SANTA CECILIA PERDIZES

State Art Gallery

AVENIDA SÃO JOÃO

Central Market

AVENIDA ANGELICA

PRAÇA DA REPÚBLICA

CENTRO

PACAEMBU

PRAÇA DE SÉ

Museum of Immigrants

AVENIDA DR. ARNALDO

RUA DE CONSOLAÇÃO

CONSOLAÇÃO

AVENIDA REBOUÇAS

Museum of the Art of São Paulo

BIXIGA

RUA 9 DE JULHO

CAMBUCI

AVENIDA DO ESTADO

JARDINS

RUA 9 DE JULHO

AVENIDA PAULISTA

LIBERDADE

AVENIDA 23 DE MAIO

ACLIMAÇÃO

AVENIDA LINS DE VASCONCELOS

RUA DOM PEDRO

R. MARIO VICENTE

PARAISO

Museum of Modern Art

VILA MARIANA

PARQUE IBIRAPUERA

Museum of São Paulo

N

very diverse: about 1.5 million inhabitants are of Italian descent, with a similar number of Spanish descent. There are also large communities from Germany (100,000), Russia (50,000), Armenia (50,000) and a further 50,000 from other Balkan and Central European countries. There is also a Japanese population of 600,000 and a Japanese district at Liberdade, south of the downtown area.

The heart of the city is pedestrianized and thronged from dawn until dusk with people going about their daily business. The first skyscraper, the Martinelli building, was only erected in 1929 but the city has expanded quickly since then. During the 1960s and 1970s the city had as many as 10,000 new residents arriving per day.

São Paulo can appear intimidating to new arrivals: an overwhelming mixture of concrete and brick, with few green spaces, due to the rapid building in the 1980s.

Despite the sprawling nature of the city, the main shopping and entertainment areas of São Paulo and the areas of historic interest are clustered around a small area between the Central Market and the Avenida Paulista.

Brasília

Since 1960 Brasília has been the capital of Brazil. It is one of the most remarkable purpose-built cities of the 20th century and contains government ministries, foreign embassies, and administrative buildings. Brasília lies in the heart of the *sertão* some 600 miles (960 km) north of Rio de Janeiro. It was built in only three years. The reason for locating the country's capital in the undeveloped plains was to encourage Brazilians to relocate there. The city now has a population of more than 1.8 million.

The Brazilian government held a competition to design the city. An urban planner, Lúcio Costa, won. He laid out the city in the shape of a bow and arrow, although some think it looks more like an airplane or bird. The main buildings were designed by the world-famous architect Oscar Niemeyer (*see* pp. 42–43).

Brasília's Eixo Monumental, or Monumental Axis. In the distance is the National Congress Building. Flanking the road are government ministry buildings.

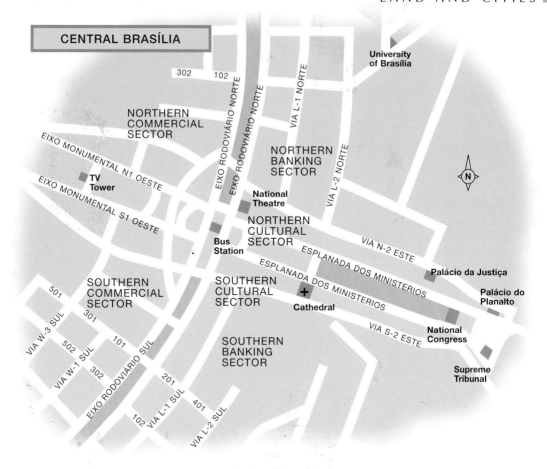

CENTRAL BRASÍLIA

University of Brasília

302   102

NORTHERN COMMERCIAL SECTOR

EIXO MONUMENTAL N1 OESTE

EIXO MONUMENTAL S1 OESTE

TV Tower

EIXO RODOVIÁRIO NORTE

EIXO RODOVIÁRIO NORTE

VIA L-1 NORTE

VIA L-2 NORTE

NORTHERN BANKING SECTOR

National Theatre

NORTHERN CULTURAL SECTOR

Bus Station

VIA N-2 ESTE

ESPLANADA DOS MINISTERIOS

ESPLANADA DOS MINISTERIOS

Palácio da Justiça

SOUTHERN COMMERCIAL SECTOR

SOUTHERN CULTURAL SECTOR

Cathedral

Palácio do Planalto

501

301

VIA W-3 SUL

502

VIA W-1 SUL

101

302

201

SOUTHERN BANKING SECTOR

VIA S-2 ESTE

National Congress

EIXO RODOVIÁRIO SUL

VIA L-1 SUL

401

102 VIA L-2 SUL

Supreme Tribunal

Brasília is spread out over a wide area. The city's *favelas* are almost 20 miles (30 km) outside the city center. The city is a vast landscape of planned plazas and long walkways separated by busy highways. Nobody walks in the city because the hot sun and lack of shade make the large distances unappealing; it was designed for the motorist.

The viewing platform at the top of the 246-foot (75-m) television tower offers a good view of the city's unusual layout. There are 19 ministry buildings (the tallest being a maximum of 28 stories) that finish in two towers. These are linked by a walkway that spells the letter H for "humanity." The most impressive of Niemeyer's futuristic-looking buildings are the twin towers of the National Congress Building with their two domes, one facing upward the other downward.

The city of Brasília abounds with symbolism. The overall shape resembles a bird or airplane. On Independence Day, the sun rises through the twin towers of the National Congress. The city's cemetery is laid out in the shape of a spiral, symbolizing the recurrent nature of life.

Oscar Niemeyer

"I sought the curved and sensual line. The curve that I see in the Brazilian hills, in the body of a loved one, in the clouds in the sky and in the ocean waves."
– Oscar Niemeyer

Oscar Niemeyer standing in front of the Double Arch at Brasília in 1986.

Born in Rio de Janeiro in 1907, Niemeyer studied at the National School of Fine Arts in Rio, at first working with Lúcio Costa, a leading Brazilian city planner and one of the foremost exponents of Modernist architecture in South America. Niemeyer was influenced by the Swiss-born French architect Le Corbusier (1887–1965), whose designs for futuristic cities had all buildings, roads, and parks integrated together. According to Le Corbusier, buildings were "machines for living in." His designs sought to exploit the possiblities offered by new building technology and what were considered industrial materials such as steel and concrete. Niemeyer worked with Le Corbusier on the education ministry building in Rio in 1936. The team also included Costa, and Robert Burle-Marx, a skilled landscape architect. Niemeyer also worked with Costa on plans for the Brazilian Pavilion at the New York World's Fair in 1939–1940.

Niemeyer's first major solo project was for Pampulha, a new suburb of Belo Horizonte for the then-mayor of the city, Juscelino Kubitschek (*see* p. 68).

(*see* p. 68).

When Kubitschek ran in the elections to become the national president, he promised Brazilians the long-dreamed-of capital city set in Brazil's interior. With a term of only five years, he knew that the project had to be finished in even less time in order for him to reap the credit. Although a public competition was held for the prestigious project, Burle-Marx said that "everyone knew in advance who was going to win." Costa's winning design is said to have consisted of a few sketches rushed out on notepaper.

Kubitschek reunited the earlier team by recruiting Niemeyer to design the new capital's major buildings. Prior to his work for Brasília, Niemeyer worked on the United Nations Building in New York City in 1947. But Brasília remains his greatest achievement. He was appointed chief architect of NOVACAP, the government building authority in Brasília from 1956 to 1961.

In the capital, Niemeyer designed the regimented ranks of the 16 identical pale-green ministries that line the boulevard approaching the parliament buildings; the Praça dos Três Poderes (the Plaza of the Three Powers, the three powers being those of the judiciary, the Congress, and the Foreign Office, whose offices stand nearby); the cathedral, its form recalling the Christian image of a crown of thorns; the university to the north; and the Palácio da Justiça (the Ministry of Justice), whose plain façade was covered with tiles by the military dictatorship in the 1960s, an embellishment that was later removed with the return to democracy.

Niemeyer integrated architecture with painting and sculpture, creating huge buildings whose environment of deserted plazas exaggerates their sculptural quality. Niemeyer's vision for Brasília was of a futuristic city that is entered and left by jet, a vision shaped by the nature of the city's location. Cut off from the rest of Brazil and miles from the nearest communications, Brasília was literally airlifted into existence.

Niemeyer returned to private practice in 1961, and with the return of an unsympathetic military government in Brazil, he moved to live in Israel and France, although he later returned to Brazil. His notable later works include the Museum of Contemporary Art near Rio (*see* p. 95) and Rio's Sambodrome, site of the city's famous samba school parade.

Niemeyer's government buildings at Brasília look out over sculpture and artificial lakes.

Salvador

Founded in 1549, the city of Salvador was the first capital of Brazil. Salvador's past as a center of trade is reflected in its splendid 17th- and 18th-century colonial architecture. Its role as the main slave port in Brazil is also reflected in the large African influence in the city's culture, cuisine, and its two million inhabitants. Salvador's wealth was built on sugar and on the slavery of the plantations. It was the center of the Recôncavo, Brazil's richest plantation zone.

The brightly colored façades of Salvador look out over the bay of Todos os Santos (All Saints).

Salvador enjoys one of the most beautiful natural harbors in the world and its brightly painted historic buildings run down a steep hill to the bay of Todos os Santos (All Saints). The city is split into two parts. The older and higher Cidade Alta (High City) is the administrative and cultural center of the city and location of its many churches. The lower Cidade Baixa (Low City) is the banking and commercial district and is largely modern, with the exception of the 16th-century fort. The two parts of the city are linked by the tall Art Deco elevator shaft built in 1930, which dominates the skyline of Salvador.

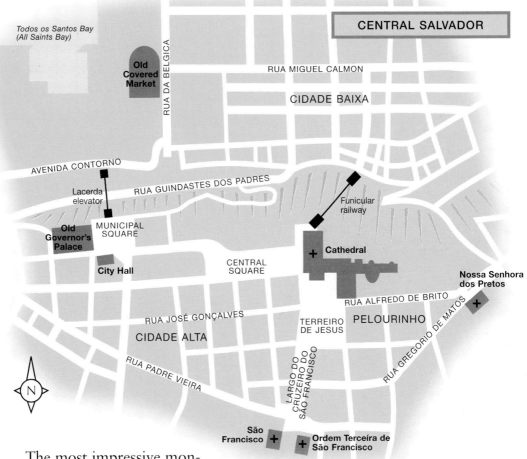

CENTRAL SALVADOR

Todos os Santos Bay
(All Saints Bay)

Old Covered Market

RUA DA BELGICA

RUA MIGUEL CALMON

CIDADE BAIXA

AVENIDA CONTORNO

Lacerda elevator

RUA GUINDASTES DOS PADRES

Funicular railway

Old Governor's Palace

MUNICIPAL SQUARE

Cathedral

Nossa Senhora dos Pretos

City Hall

CENTRAL SQUARE

RUA ALFREDO DE BRITO

RUA JOSÉ GONÇALVES

CIDADE ALTA

TERREIRO DE JESUS

PELOURINHO

RUA GREGORIO DE MATOS

RUA PADRE VIEIRA

LARGO DO CRUZEIRO DO SÃO FRANCISCO

N

São Francisco

Ordem Terceíra de São Francisco

The most impressive monuments in Salvador are the churches built during the colonial period. Of these the most beautiful is probably the elaborately carved Igreja da Ordem Terceíra de São Francisco, but the most popular is the Igreja do Nosso Senhor do Bonfim in Salvador's suburbs, a site of pilgrimage famous throughout Brazil.

The area of Pelourinho in the center of the Cidade Alta has recently been renovated by the local government, the ornate façades of its colonial buildings repainted in the bright colors for which the city is famous.

Salvador has a rich cultural life. It is home to the music of *tropicalismo*, and the birthplace of many of Brazil's most respected writers and artists. It is also the center of *candomblé* religion (*see* p. 114) and has a vibrant annual carnival which many feel rivals Rio's.

Most of the population of Salvador lives in the higher Cidade Alta, which overlooks the bay to the east.

Past and Present

"Brazil grows in the dark while its politicians sleep."

Brazilian saying

Little is known of Brazil's prehistory or of the people who lived in the country before the arrival of European colonialists in the late 15th century. Thereafter, Brazil's history has been the history of its trade with the rest of the world, because the development of Brazil has largely been shaped by the nature of that trade.

The first attraction of Brazil for European colonialists was the brazil wood grown there and used to dye the textiles of northern Europe. This crop was soon supplanted by sugar. Massive, highly profitable sugar plantations led to a scramble among the European powers for Brazilian territory and to the enslavement of the native people and of people transported from Africa. The use of oxen on the plantations led to cattle ranching and the opening up of the Brazilian interior. This in turn led to the discovery of gold and diamonds and the beginnings of mining in Minas Gerais. The continual opening up of Brazil's "Wild West" led, as in North America, to the formation of unique, independent communities.

Starting in the 1820s a coffee boom fueled the rapid development of the southeastern cities of Rio and São Paulo and laid the foundations for the industrialization that was to follow in the 20th century. Attempts have been made since the 1950s to open up the country further with a series of road-building projects which aimed to distribute industry, and wealth, more evenly.

Celebrations for the victory of Tancredo Neves in 1985, the first democratically elected president since the 1960s. He died before taking office.

THE FIRST PEOPLES

Brazil's earliest inhabitants settled there between 10,000 and 5,000 years ago. They were nomadic hunter-gatherers. They moved around in search of food, timing their moves to coincide with the flooding of the Amazon River. They learned to live in harmony with their environment, using the forest's rich resources without causing any long-term damage. Manioc, or cassava (a starchy root crop), was an important source of food, as were fish and small mammals. Over time, these people discovered how to use the leaves and bark of different trees to make medicines, such as quinine and cocaine.

These early people of Brazil did not develop civilizations like those of the Maya of Mexico and Guatemala and the Inca of Peru. They lived in small, mobile groups. Different groups were at almost constant warfare with one other. They fought fiercely with clubs and bows, and captured enemies were killed and eaten. They had few possessions and have left little for archaeologists to discover. The most advanced societies seem to have been developed on the large river island of Marajó at the mouth of the Amazon River. There, archaeologists have found fragments of ceramic pots that are around 8,000 years old—the oldest known pottery of the Americas.

Around 7000 to 4000 B.C., the temperature rose in southern Brazil, causing the groups of people living there to move to the cooler coasts. These people lived on shellfish; mounds of shells—some as tall as 80 feet (25 m) high—

This ceramic funerary urn was found on the island of Marajó in the Amazon. It was produced between A.D. 400 and 700 and was used to preserve human bones, through which it was believed the living could contact the dead.

Brazil's Native Peoples c. 1500

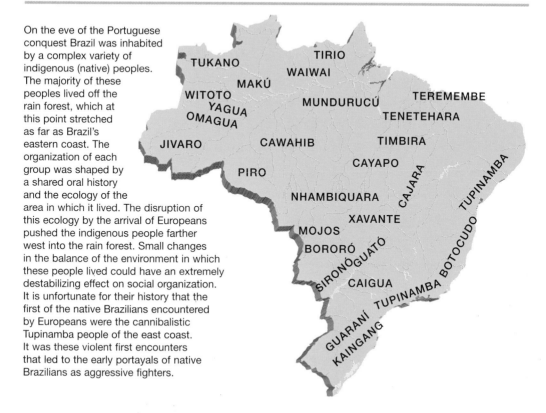

On the eve of the Portuguese conquest Brazil was inhabited by a complex variety of indigenous (native) peoples. The majority of these peoples lived off the rain forest, which at this point stretched as far as Brazil's eastern coast. The organization of each group was shaped by a shared oral history and the ecology of the area in which it lived. The disruption of this ecology by the arrival of Europeans pushed the indigenous people farther west into the rain forest. Small changes in the balance of the environment in which these people lived could have an extremely destabilizing effect on social organization. It is unfortunate for their history that the first of the native Brazilians encountered by Europeans were the cannibalistic Tupinamba people of the east coast. It was these violent first encounters that led to the early portayals of native Brazilians as aggressive fighters.

TUKANO
TIRIO
WAIWAI
MAKÚ
WITOTO
YAGUA
OMAGUA
MUNDURUCÚ
TEREMEMBE
TENETEHARA
JIVARO
CAWAHIB
TIMBIRA
CAYAPO
PIRO
CAJARA
TUPINAMBA
NHAMBIQUARA
XAVANTE
MOJOS
BORORÓ
SIRONÓ
GUATÓ
BOTOCUDO
CAIGUA
GUARANÍ
TUPINAMBA
KAINGANG

have been discovered by archaeologists.

By 100 to 200 B.C., native peoples had settled throughout Brazil, living in communities that stayed in one location rather than moving from place to place as their ancestors had done. These people formed communities no larger than a few local villages.

By the time of the Portuguese arrival in the 16th century, Brazil had an estimated population of about two to five million people. At this time, some groups had settled into chiefdoms, led by a chieftain who governed one or more villages. One example was the village of Teso dos Bichos on Marajó Island at the mouth of the Amazon. Archaeologists think that the village was inhabited continually for around 900 years by between 500 and 1,000 people who lived in houses made out of earth, wooden poles, and thatch.

When the Portuguese landed in Brazil in 1500, it is estimated that there were about five million native people living there. Today there are only about 220,000.

The Portuguese Empire

In the 15th century, Portugal built up a vast overseas empire. Its rival in empire building was its neighbor, Spain. The kings and queens of both countries sent fleets of ships, led by skilled navigators, in search of new, speedier trading routes to the spice-rich Indies. During their long journeys, the navigators often inadvertently came across new lands, whose territories they claimed for their mother countries. While Spain was exploring the islands of the Caribbean, the Portuguese were sailing around Africa, setting up trading stations along the coast. In 1498, the Portuguese explorer Vasco da Gama reached India. Later, Portugal built an empire in the East Indies, exploiting the lucrative spice trade.

Both Spain and Portugal were Roman Catholic nations. Their kings recognized the pope in Rome as their spiritual and political leader. In an attempt to cool their intense rivalry, the pope oversaw a treaty between them. The Treaty of Tordesilhas of 1494 ceded Brazil to Portugal, although at this stage the Portuguese had still to set foot in the country. Portugal lost much of its empire to the Dutch and the British during the 17th and 18th centuries, but its last African colonies (Angola, Guinea Bissau, and Mozambique) were not given their independence until the mid-1970s

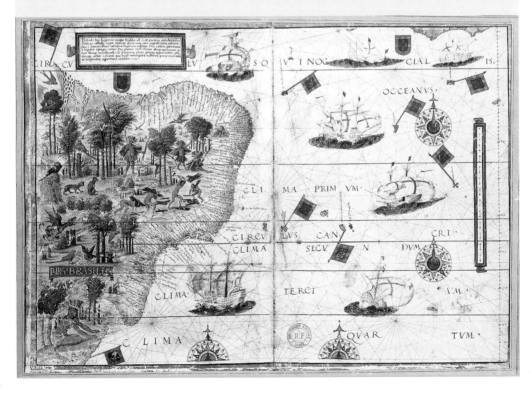

A COLONY OF PORTUGAL

In the late 15th century, European expeditions, including those of Amerigo Vespucci and Diego de Lepe, sailed along the Brazilian coast and made landfall. Today, however, both the Portuguese and Brazilians celebrate the Portuguese navigator Pedro Álvares Cabral (1467/8–1520) as the first European to set foot in Brazil.

The "Island of the True Cross"

In 1499, Cabral set sail from Portugal on a trading mission to India. He sailed down past northern Africa to the continent's southern tip. Before reaching the Cape of Good Hope at the southern tip of Africa, strong currents carried his ships

EARLY EUROPEAN EXPEDITIONS TO SOUTH AMERICA

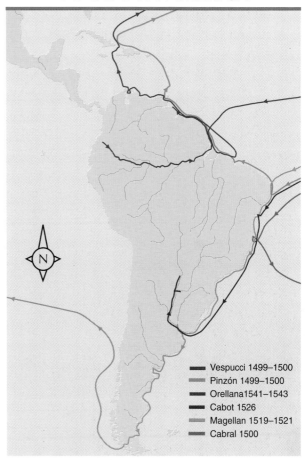

- ▬ Vespucci 1499–1500
- ▬ Pinzón 1499–1500
- ▬ Orellana1541–1543
- ▬ Cabot 1526
- ▬ Magellan 1519–1521
- ▬ Cabral 1500

westward. Some people think that Cabral sailed west deliberately because he was on a secret mission from the Portuguese king. In all events, on April 22, 1500, Cabral sighted land—Mount Pascal in Brazil. Two days later, he landed at present-day Pôrto Seguro, south of Itabuna, where he encountered friendly native peoples. He thought the land he had reached was an island. He called it the "Island of the True Cross" because it was Eastertime. The Portuguese remained for just nine days before setting sail again. They carried with them logs from the brazil-wood tree, which, they discovered, produced a striking red dye. They called the wood

The Spanish crown funded the expeditions of Orellana, Pinzón, the Venetian Cabot, the Florentine Vespucci, and the Portuguese Magellan. Only Cabral sailed under the flag of the Portuguese crown.

pau-brasil because it was the color of glowing embers, *brasa* in Portuguese. Later, the country took its name from the trees.

Cabral's landfall gave the Portuguese a foothold in the Americas. At the time, however, the explorer did not know that he had arrived on the continent. Only later explorations revealed that the "island" of Brazil was in fact part of a huge landmass and that Portugal and Spain were rivals for the same territory.

Pedro Alvares Cabral

Born at Belmonte in Portugal in 1467/8, the son of a nobleman, Cabral enjoyed the favor of King Manuel. In 1499, he was appointed admiral in command of 13 ships that set sail along Vasco da Gama's route for India. Sailing southwest to take advantage of the current, he was carried off course and discovered Brazil. After only nine days in Brazil, Cabral sailed for India, losing four ships at the southern tip of Africa before casting anchor in India at Calicut. Disputes with Muslim traders led to a bombardment by the Portuguese. Cabral lost a further four ships on the route home. Thereafter, despite finding favor with the king, Cabral was passed over in place of his rival da Gama and he retired to his estate in the Beira Baixa province of Portugal, where he died in 1520.

Degredados and Captains

Back in Portugal, the brazil wood attracted the interest of a few merchants. Having gained the rights to deal in the brazil-wood trade, they set up trading stations along the Brazilian coast. At the time, the Portuguese empire was vast, stretching from West Africa via India to Asia. The "island" of Brazil was not considered an important part of the Portuguese empire and was ignored by the authorities. Few Europeans settled there, other than a few petty criminals and outcasts—called *degredados* by the Portuguese. The *degredados* learned the native languages of Brazil and sometimes married chieftains' daughters. Their mixed-race children are often called the first Brazilians.

Soon French and British traders began to take an interest in the lucrative brazil-wood trade. They seized Portuguese ships and traded directly with the native people. In 1530, the Portuguese king, realizing that he might lose this new territory, decided to set up a royal colony in Brazil, at São Vicente. Because of the size of its empire, however, the Portuguese crown could not afford to run the colony directly. Instead, the king divided the Brazilian coast into 12 regions and gave each region to a Portuguese nobleman.

The new rulers—called donatary captains—were given a lot of power but usually failed to make their private colonies prosper. Exasperated, the Portuguese king reasserted his power over Brazil by sending a governor-general to oversee the captains. He set up his government at Salvador, the first capital of Brazil.

The first capital of Brazil after the arrival of the Europeans was set up at Salvador in Bahia in 1549. It remained the capital for the next 214 years, until it moved to Rio de Janeiro in the 18th century.

Sugar and the Rise of Slavery

In the 1550s, the Portuguese started to set up sugar-cane plantations in northeast Brazil. Portugal had set up similar plantations in other parts of its empire, in the Azores and Madeira. Sugar quickly replaced brazil wood as the colony's main export.

Sugar cultivation was very labor intensive. Each plantation needed between 100 and 150 skilled and unskilled workers. The native peoples had been happy to trade with the Portuguese, but they did not want to

This contemporary French print shows native Brazilians attacking colonial villages in the early French and Portuguese colonization of Brazil. Such documents did much to create the European belief that the native peoples were savages.

Bandeirantes and Jesuits

During the 17th and 18th centuries, raiders known as *bandeirantes* marched into the interior of Brazil to capture and enslave the native Brazilians. The raiders got their name from *bandeira*, the Portuguese word for "flag." Most *bandeirantes* were born of native mothers and Portuguese fathers and spoke both a native language and Portuguese.

The *bandeirantes* traveled for years at a time in groups of 12 to 200 men. They plundered native villages and captured their inhabitants for the sugar plantations. Jesuit missionaries, who had arrived to convert the native Brazilians to Christianity, tried to protect them from the *bandeirantes*. They built missions in the remotest parts of Brazil and armed the natives. Although the *bandeirantes* were slowed down, the Jesuits never succeeded in stopping the raids. Instead, the settlers captured the missions and, with the help of the Portuguese and Spanish rulers in Europe—now disturbed at the extent of Jesuit power in Brazil—the Jesuits were finally expelled from Brazil in 1759.

work on the sugar plantations. Portuguese traders and the Catholic clergy thought that the native peoples were lazy. They began to seize the natives and forced them to work on the plantations as slaves.

At the same time, the Portuguese king sent religious missionaries of a Roman Catholic order called Jesuits to convert the natives to Christianity and to help keep the peace between the Portuguese settlers and the natives. The Jesuits set up missionary settlements, called *aldeias*, where they tried to convert the natives. They quickly met opposition from the settlers, including their priests, who saw the Jesuits' activities as hindering the prosperity of the plantations. Much of the early history of the colony was marked by conflict beween the Jesuits and the settlers and their competing aims.

The Empire Is Threatened

When the popularity of sugar took off in Europe in the early 17th century, other European countries also tried to establish colonies in what later became the valuable real estate of northeastern Brazil. In the 1550s, 500 Protestants from France settled at Guanabara Bay—an area visited but not settled by the Portuguese. They called their colony France Antarctique. The Portuguese sent ships down to the French colony and finally ousted the French in 1567. They founded their own city there—Rio de Janeiro.

Later the Dutch, too, threatened the Portuguese colony. In 1630, they seized the prosperous settlement of Pernambuco—a rich area of sugarcane plantations. With

the prosperous Dutch navy much stronger than that of the Portuguese, it seemed as if the Portuguese empire would collapse. The Portuguese fought back, however, recapturing Pernambuco in 1654. The Dutch settlers of Brazil went to the Caribbean, where they founded a rival sugarcane industry. From then on the Portuguese were the masters of Brazil.

A depiction of a 17th-century sugar plantation in Brazil held by the Dutch West Indian Company. The Dutch held parts of northeastern Brazil but were soon to move their colonial attentions to the islands of the Caribbean.

African Slavery

After colonization, the native peoples died in huge numbers. Lacking any resistance to European diseases such as measles, they died whenever they contracted any European disease. In epidemics that raged in 1562 and 1563, one-third of the native peoples living in the coastal area died.

Faced with a shortage of native labor, the Portuguese started to bring slaves from Africa to work on the sugar plantations. Throughout the 17th century, black slaves replaced native people on the plantations. Life was hard.

The slaves worked a 15- to 17-hour day, and lived in filthy, disease-ridden conditions. So many died that the Portuguese had to keep importing replacements. Historians estimate that of the ten million black African slaves who survived the long Atlantic crossing to the Americas, 40 percent were sent to Brazil. Up to 13 million men, women, and children were imported into Brazil during 350 years of slavery. More slaves were imported to Brazil than to any other nation—almost six times the number taken to the United States.

A 17th-century depiction of a Brazilian slave market from the notebook of Zacharias Wagner, painted during his stay at the court of the Brazilian governor.

The large numbers of black people in Brazil quickly led to a very racially mixed population. In addition to whites, blacks, and natives, there were mulattos or *pardos* (black-white), *caboclos* (white-native), and *cafusos* (native-black). In Brazilian society, skin color became important because it determined a person's social status.

The *Quilombos*

The history of slavery in Brazil is filled with rebellions and uprisings. The terrible conditions on the sugar plantations and, later, in the gold mines, led many slaves to attempt escape. *Quilombos*—free territories—were set up all over Brazil by runaway slaves. The Portuguese plantation and mine owners wanted the *quilombos* destroyed at all costs and made special efforts to portray them as dangerous places.

The most famous and longest-surviving *quilombo*, the Republic of Palmares, lasted from 1630 to 1695, and comprised 30,000 people headed by their leader Zumbi. They lived in dozens of villages scattered over some 17,000 square miles (over 44,000 sq. km) in central Brazil. Because men far outnumbered women in the *quilombo*, it was not unusual for a woman to have up to five husbands. The ex-slaves lived a typical village life of their time. They hunted, fished, farmed, and made pottery, musical instruments, baskets, clothing, and weapons with which to defend themselves. For the Portuguese, the existence of the Republic of Palmares was an incitement to other slaves to revolt. The Portuguese wanted Zumbi killed and the *quilombo* destroyed.

After several attempts, the colonial government finally succeeded in killing Zumbi and overthrew Palmares in 1695. They put Zumbi's severed head on a pole as a warning to all slaves. The warning failed; slaves continued to escape. Today Zumbi is an official national hero of Brazil.

Gold and the Expanding Colony

For a long time, the *bandeirantes* and the Jesuits were the only whites or mulattos to venture into Brazil's interior. In the mid-17th century, as the slave trade dwindled, the *bandeirantes* began to search for precious minerals. The Spanish crown, after all, had grown rich on the New World silver from Potosí in Bolivia. In the 1690s, *bandeirantes* struck gold in an area north of São Paulo, later known as Minas Gerais ("General Mines").

Encouraged, the *bandeirantes* pushed farther into the interior. They discovered new gold deposits at Mato Grosso and Goiás. Diamonds, too, were discovered in the area later known as Diamantina. Owing to the explorations of the *bandeirantes*, Brazil's frontiers now stretched hundreds of miles west beyond the line

The gold rush shifted Brazil's center of wealth from the sugar plantations of the northeast to the mines of the southeast. Accordingly, in 1763 the capital was moved from Salvador to Rio.

BRAZIL'S ECONOMY IN THE 16TH AND 17TH CENTURIES

16TH CENTURY

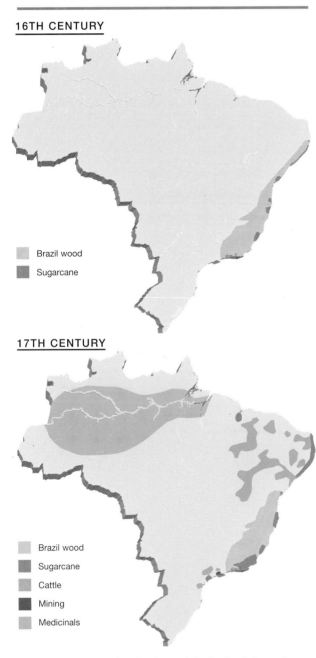

Brazil wood

Sugarcane

17TH CENTURY

Brazil wood

Sugarcane

Cattle

Mining

Medicinals

Forestry and cattle farming formed the basis of the early Brazilian economy. Sugar farming spread from the northeast to become Brazil's dominant cash crop.

established under the Treaty of Tordesilhas demarcating the border between Spanish and Portuguese territories. The Spanish king did nothing, however. In 1750, under the Treaty of Madrid, Spain recognized Brazil's borders. Brazil's economy flourished and soon became far richer than that of Portugal itself.

The discovery of gold brought thousands of new immigrants to Brazil. Over 400,000 Portuguese came to Brazil on news of the gold rush, and the population boomed. In 1710, the colony's population stood at 30,000. By 1800, it was half a million. The statistics are extraordinary. Between 1700 and 1820, 1,200 tons of gold were mined in Minas Gerais; this constituted 80 percent of all the gold mined in the world during the period. Mining brought immense wealth to the region, making its inhabitants some of the richest people on earth. New settlements sprang up in the gold-mining areas. The settlements often grew very rich and their inhabitants were able to build lavish mansions and churches. Settlers resented the royal government in Rio de Janeiro and the high taxes they had to pay.

Ouro Prêto

The most prosperous town of all was Ouro Prêto, in Minas Gerais. Its name means "Black Gold," referring to the gold discovered here, discolored by iron ore. It was at Ouro Prêto that the first attempt was made to free Brazil from the rule of the Portuguese king and make the colony a republic (*see* box). Because many of the miners had started their own businesses and were used to working for themselves, the town gained a taste for democracy; this contrasted with the interests of absent wealthy landowners in other parts of the country, who built vast fortunes from the labor of others.

The baroque church of Nossa Senhora do Carmo overlooks the town of Ouro Prêto.

Tiradentes

In the late 1780s, a group of prominent citizens of Ouro Prêto, including lawyers, landowners, and a priest, started to plot in secret for Brazilian independence. The conspirators were betrayed and the Portuguese king decided to make an example of them.

One of the principal conspirators was a young army officer, Joaquim José da Silva Xavier, better known by his nickname "Tiradentes" ("toothpuller")— he also worked as a dentist. Tiradentes wanted Brazilian independence, which, he also believed, would mean an end to slavery. The authorities considered Tiradentes the ringleader. Along with his fellow conspirators, Tiradentes waited in prison for two years while the royal government prepared the case against them. Finally, all the conspirators were sentenced to death. Queen Dona Maria I, however, reduced the death sentence to exile for all except Tiradentes. He was executed in April 1792 and a curse placed on his descendants. Today, Brazilians celebrate Tiradentes as a national hero and the curse on his family has been lifted.

King Dom João VI of Portugal whose love of Brazil led to it being elevated to a kingdom in 1816 and to its independence under his son in 1822.

Moves Toward Independence

For a time, hopes for an independent Brazil seemed futile. The country had little separate identity, and there was no university or printing press to spread new ideas. It was events in Europe that led to Brazilian independence. In 1807, the French emperor Napoleon marched into Portugal and captured its capital, Lisbon, for his empire. The king, Dom João VI (1767–1826), fled. He and his court of some 15,000 people sailed for Rio de Janeiro under the protection of the British navy. Rio de Janeiro suddenly became the capital of a world empire. Dom João fell in love with the handsome city and stayed in Brazil long after Napoleon was defeated in 1814. In 1820, Portugal underwent a liberal revolution and a constitutional monarchy was declared. The new government summoned the king home as head of state. Dom João left Brazil in 1821. Fearing he might lose control of the colony, he left his son Pedro (1798–1834) behind as prince regent (the son of a king who rules in his father's place).

The Portuguese government wanted to make Brazil a colony again. The prince regent refused to accept this. In 1822, on the banks of the Ipiranga River, he uttered the famous cry for Brazilian independence *"Independência ou morte!"* ("Independence or death!"). It is now known as the *Grito de Ipiranga*. Pedro was crowned Brazil's first emperor and ruled for the next nine years. By 1824, the emperor had asserted his rule over the whole of Brazil. He set up a constitution establishing a parliamentary government with two chambers—a senate whose members were chosen by the emperor and a chamber of deputies whose members were elected by the country's wealthy and influential men. Under the constitution, the emperor remained powerful. In 1825, Portugal, urged on by its ally Great Britain, recognized Brazil's independence.

In return for Britain's help, in 1826 Brazil agreed to give the British special trading rights and promised to abolish the slave trade within three years.

Both the Brazilian aristocracy and the people were very suspicious of the emperor, believing he favored Portuguese inhabitants over native Brazilians. Other Brazilians wanted to make Brazil a republic. Uprisings and rebellions were a common feature of the emperor's rule. These were largely slaves rising against masters, and Indian and mixed-race Brazilians fighting against white domination. One of the first revolts was the Cabanagem Rebellion in the state of Pará, where many poor people rose against their masters in 1835. The rebels captured Belém and the governor was killed. The uprising sparked off other revolts in the Amazon region. Another began in Maranhão in 1838. The city of Caxias was captured by rebels and held for three years. Other revolts took place in Bahia, Pernambuco, and Rio Grande do Sul during the 1830s and 1840s.

BRAZIL'S ECONOMY IN THE 18TH AND 19TH CENTURIES

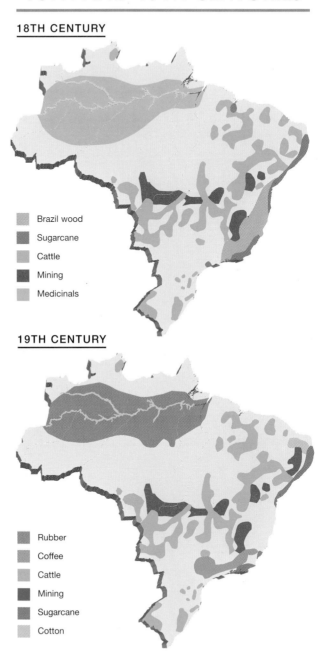

18TH CENTURY

- Brazil wood
- Sugarcane
- Cattle
- Mining
- Medicinals

19TH CENTURY

- Rubber
- Coffee
- Cattle
- Mining
- Sugarcane
- Cotton

Gold was first discovered by the bandeirantes in 1695 and its exploitation boosted Brazilian industry, providing the infrastructure for the later booms in rubber and coffee.

Finally, Dom Pedro was forced to give up his throne in favor of his five-year-old son, Pedro (1825–1841). Without a strong leader, rival parties fought to control Brazil. There were wars and rebellions throughout the country, and it even seemed that the country would fall apart. Finally, it was decided that in the interests of the country the young Pedro should take the throne. He was just 14 years old.

Dom Pedro II

Dom Pedro II took control of Brazil in 1840, He ruled for half a century, and his reign was the most prosperous period in Brazil's history thus far. He managed to reconcile the interests of the conservative province of Rio de Janeiro—the seat of the government—with the wealthy, more forward-thinking provinces of Minas Gereis and São Paulo.

During the American Civil War, Abraham Lincoln declared that King Pedro of Brazil was the only man he could trust to negotiate between the northern and southern states of the United States.

Dom Pedro was a complex character. On the one hand, he was a great supporter of modern technology. Brazil was the second country after Britain to introduce the postage stamp. Dom Pedro was the first Brazilian to have a telephone, and he encouraged the expansion of the railroads. In other ways, however, the emperor refused to move with the times. For a long time, he resisted attempts to carry out his father's promise to abolish slavery. His other major failing was allowing the military to direct foreign policy. His generals plunged Brazil into a disastrous war with Paraguay, the War of the Triple Alliance—an alliance consisting of the combined forces of Brazil, Argentina, and Uruguay. The war lasted from 1864 to 1870 and resulted in the loss of 100,000 Brazilian lives

Slavery and the Coffee Boom

In the 19th century, coffee replaced sugar, cotton, and gold as the chief Brazilian export. In the 1850s and 1860s, there was a coffee boom. Immigrants flooded in from Europe, drawn by the new wealth of Rio, São

Paulo, and Minas Gerais. Slaves were still used on the coffee plantations, despite protests from Britain. The British navy was able to put a stop to the Atlantic slave trade, but a decision to bring an end to slavery within Brazil had to come from Brazilians themselves. Over the decades, more and more Brazilians recognized that slavery had to be ended. In 1888, a law abolishing slavery went before the Brazilian parliament and was passed almost unanimously. Most Latin American countries had become republics and Brazilians, still subject to a monarchy, fell out of step with their neighbors. The antislavery movement was a key part in the increasing rejection of the constitutional monarchy in the 1870s and 1880s. Pedro's problems grew as economic recession, financial problems, the interference of the Catholic church in affairs of state, and low morale among the Brazilian military officers pushed the republicans into action.

A Berlin coffeehouse during the 19th century. The growth in European coffee-drinking provided a huge boost to the Brazilian economy.

INDEPENDENCE

As with the rest of Brazil's history, the country's achievement of independence was unique in Latin America by being entirely peaceful. On November 15, 1889, a bloodless military coup deposed the emperor, who went into exile. A new constitution was adopted. It ensured that the church no longer played a part in government, introduced the right to vote for any literate male (about 3 percent of the total population), and established a federal system in which each province governed itself as a state in its own right in a way similar to the United States. The changes were symbolized on the new Brazilian flag by the words "Order and Progress."

This 19th-century mansion in the Tijuca Forest near Rio de Janeiro is typical of the large properties built by the rich owners of the coffee plantations.

The First Republic

Because of their economic power, the coffee growers of São Paulo, along with the cattle farmers of Minas Gerais, dominated the politics of the new republic. Known as the *café com leite* (coffee and milk alliance), they split power between them, with the military acting as the intermediary, much as the monarchy had previously done. Within the terms of the new constitution military intervention in the government had been made illegal. Political instability, however, led the military to take control of government.

By the 1920s the tensions between the coffee growers of São Paulo and the cattle ranchers of Minas Gerais were out in the open. The

The Rubber Boom

The Amazon rubber boom of the 19th century was Brazil's most dramatic experience of boom-and-bust. The naturally growing rubber tree of the *várzea* became highly prized in Europe and the United States after a Scotsman, John Dunlop, devised a practical rubber tire in 1888 for the growing auto industry. The price for natural rubber soared overnight and Amazon rubber plantation owners, using slave labor, set about supplying the demand of the industrialized nations.

A spectacular economic boom followed. By 1900, the remote port town of Manaus, 1,000 miles (1,600 km) from the Atlantic Ocean, was fantastically rich. Manaus modeled itself on a European city, even building a famous opera house, Teatro Amazonas, which drew operatic performers from Europe. The theater took 17 years to build at a cost of $3 million and still stands today.

So rich were the plantation owners that they sent their laundry to Portugal to be cleaned! The workers on the rubber plantations never benefited from the rubber boom.

The boom ended as abruptly as it had started. An Englishman, Henry Wickham, smuggled rubber-plant seeds out of Brazil and botanists in London's Kew Gardens used them to grow seedlings that were exported to the British colonies in Malaysia and India. The efficiently run Asian plantations produced many more trees than Brazil. Increased supply caused the price of rubber to drop and by the 1920s the boom had ended and Manaus had lost its world importance.

In 1926, Henry Ford, in trying to provide his own rubber source for the Ford Motor Company's production of tires, set up a rubber plantation in Amazonia called Fordlândia. The plantation failed.

cattle ranchers resented the coffee growers for artificially inflating the price of coffee during periods of over-supply. Other groups were also restless and junior military officers launched unsuccessful coups in 1922, 1924, and 1926.

Following the end of World War I (1914–1918), the United States rose to world power status while Britain declined. Brazil was still exporting almost all its produce to Europe at low prices. Its economy suffered even before the collapse of share prices on Wall Street in 1929, which led to the withdrawal of American investment. This resulted in Brazil setting aside most of its revenue to pay its mounting debt. Amid the financial chaos, a desire for economic and national independence grew.

Getúlio Vargas and the Estado Nôvo

The period from 1930 to 1945 was a defining period in Brazilian history. It ended the control of the government by the São Paulo coffee growers and saw the economic basis of the country shift from export-led growth to the government investing in industry. The man behind these changes was Getúlio Vargas, who became the model for Brazilian politics for the rest of the 20th century (*see* box opposite), when government alternated between political leaders supported by the people and rule by the military. Labor legislation was the key to Vargas' success. He realized Brazil was becoming increasingly industrialized and passed laws to create a social welfare system and to legalize labor unions. Working Brazilians found them- selves with paid vacation time and a minimum wage, but were banned from going on strike. Vargas' rule became more dictatorial after 1937 and his secret police tortured political prisoners who were his opponents.

Economic pressure forced Vargas to join the Allies against Germany in 1942, but the demand of Allied forces for Brazilian rubber boosted the Brazilian economy. Meanwhile, Brazil's ally, the United States, invested heavily in the new Brazilian steel industry. Vargas oversaw the establishment of state corporations such as the national petroleum company, Petrobras. Peasants flocked to expanding cities such as São Paulo.

Vargas' support lay with the urban working class and he earned their allegiance by nationalizing (bringing into public ownership) the oil, electricity, and steel industries. His political allies were young, energetic administrators who sought to bring the Brazilian economy into line with 20th-century industry, by abandoning the vested interests of the old coffee producers and cattle farmers and governing in favor of the whole economy rather than a

Latin America was hit sharply by the world depression after 1929. Many governments were discredited and in the years 1930 and 1931, 11 out of the 20 republics of Latin America had revolutions. In most cases populist dictators, such as Vargas in Brazil, took charge.

Getúlio Vargas

Vargas was born in 1883 in São Borja in Rio Grande do Sul. He was a *caudillo* (strong man) in the Latin American tradition, who turned his country into a dictatorship. A wealthy rancher, he served as the governor of Rio Grande do Sul for two years before, backed by the military, he seized the presidency in 1930. Initially, he was Brazil's most popular leader since Dom Pedro II. His supporters were in the growing urban working and middle classes that had not been represented in Brazilian politics until Vargas came to power. Despite his popularity, Vargas did not allow Brazil to become more democratic. Instead, he manipulated Congress to keep himself in power in 1937 and was saved from growing opposition in 1942 by declaring war against Germany. When the military removed him from power in 1945 he retired, only to be reelected in 1950.

Vargas was accused of trying to murder one of his chief political opponents, and on August 24, 1954, he shot himself rather than be forced to resign. After his death, Brazilians came to regard him as one of their great presidents.

few landowners. The administration was hardly democratic, but it did spread Brazil's wealth more evenly.

The Second Republic 1946–1964

Improvements made to the average Brazilian's working life could not offset state repression and corruption. Initially, Vargas had relied on the military's support but, with a decline in his public support, they made him resign in 1945. His popularity returned though. He was elected president in 1950 for his third presidential term, during which he committed suicide. His final term was beset by financial difficulties and opposition to foreign investment. He tried to reconcile nationalist calls for economic

During the building of Brasília, President Kubitschek spent almost every weekend at the new city, overseeing planning and building work.

independence and foreign demands for returns on investments, particularly from the United States.

Following Vargas' suicide, Brazil's next president was Juscelino Kubitschek, who took office in 1956. An optimist who believed Brazil needed to expand economically as quickly as possible, he devised the slogan "Fifty years in five." Kubitschek is best remembered for the building of the new capital, Brasília (*see* pp. 40–41). The cost of building the new city sent Brazil spiraling into debt and the next president, Jânio Quadros, had to resign after only seven months of his presidency because of Brazil's economic problems. Power passed to his vice-president, João Goulart, whose populism caused both the right wing and the army to distrust him. Goulart had the support of military units in his home state of Rio Grande do Sul, and, fearing a civil war, the military agreed to a compromise, allowing Goulart to assume the presidency, but with greatly reduced powers.

The 1960s were turbulent times for Brazil, as they were for much of Latin America. Following the 1959 Cuban Revolution, the United States, wary of another revolution within the American continent, launched the Alliance for Progress in 1961, which allowed for increased U.S. involvement in Latin America. American volunteers flooded into the continent: Brazil received more than 600. Within Brazilian universities, the effects of the Cuban Revolution were felt as students took up the call for revolution and backed peasants' demands for land reform. Inflation continued to soar and, when President Goulart introduced social and political reforms, including land distribution to the peasants, giving voting rights to 20 million illiterate Brazilians and legalising the communist party, it became clear that the military would try to oppose such liberal policies.

Military Rule 1964–1985

When the coup came in 1964 it was backed by the Brazilian middle classes and by the United States. At first, Brazil's military regime was not as brutal as others, such as those in Chile and Argentina. Unlike other Latin American military dictators such as Chile's General Pinochet and Paraguay's Alfredo Stroessner, Brazilian military generals stuck to their four-year terms in office.

The generals' avowed aim was to "restore democracy,

Attempts at revolution in the postwar period and the rise of left-wing guerrilla groups in the 1960s and 1970s led the military to seize power in much of South America, largely supported by the middle classes.

POLITICAL INSTABILITY IN SOUTH AMERICA

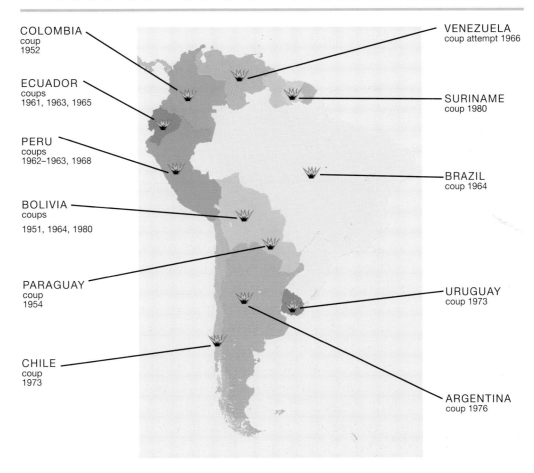

COLOMBIA
coup
1952

ECUADOR
coups
1961, 1963, 1965

PERU
coups
1962–1963, 1968

BOLIVIA
coups
1951, 1964, 1980

PARAGUAY
coup
1954

CHILE
coup
1973

VENEZUELA
coup attempt 1966

SURINAME
coup 1980

BRAZIL
coup 1964

URUGUAY
coup 1973

ARGENTINA
coup 1976

reduce inflation, and end corruption." Instead, democratic organizations were banned, corruption became common, strong press censorship was used, and, when the generals fell from power, they left a huge, unpayable foreign debt. However, for a period during the late 1960s and early 1970s it seemed as if military rule had performed an economic miracle. The economy had grown by over 10 percent each year, and the change from a rural to a semi-industrialized country speeded up.

Tanks and combat troops surround the Laranjeiras Palace Rio, where President Goulart was staying in spring 1964, during the military coup.

Grand Projects

The lack of any land redistribution led millions of peasants to move to cities, creating the *favelas*. Diverting attention from the lack of land reform, the military government set about developing the Amazon region (an act that led directly to deforestation). The opening-up of the Amazon region was representative of the shortsighted but large-scale projects the military undertook to deflect attention from much-needed social reforms. Meanwhile, as the economy boomed between 1968 and 1973, the middle classes had never had it so good. However, wealth became increasingly concentrated in their hands and the inequality that still blights Brazil today grew more apparent. As Brazil emerged as a world power and the dominant economic power of Latin America, home opposition to military dictatorship grew. The military became more repressive. Historians estimate that 20,000 Brazilians were imprisoned, most were tortured, and many killed. State control of the media meant that accurate figures were never obtained.

The Campaign for Democracy

A series of strikes began in São Paulo with the metalworkers in 1977 and spread throughout the city's industrial belt. The strikes were illegal—unions having been banned under military rule—but the workers were led by the charismatic factory worker Lula (Luis Inácio da Silva) under whom they achieved widespread support. Such was the importance of the São Paulo region for the Brazilian economy that the generals realized further disruption would be disastrous for the whole country. Organized labor was accepted and the challenge to the military appeared to have succeeded.

This was combined with the mass Campaign for Direct Elections in the years 1983 to 1984. In the early 1980s, reforms led to the end of censorship and saw the return of many exiled politicians. In the first presidential elections, however, the military insisted that the president be chosen by an electoral college nominated by the military-dominated Congress. Vast rallies of over a million people in Rio and São Paulo demanded "democracy now." It was only with the emergence of Tancredo Neves that a coalition of democrats and the military managed to save the situation.

Transition to Democracy

When the military handed power back to civilian rule, Brazil was a greatly changed nation. By 1985, the economy had grown to become the tenth largest in the world, but wages, health, and education levels for all except the elite had failed to keep pace with the growth. Society was more unequal and corrupt and political institutions weakened. Only a gradual ten-year transition from military to civilian rule prevented political upheaval and trials of the military for the abuse of human rights.

RETURN TO CIVILIAN RULE

While the economy boomed, the Brazilian middle class accepted military rule. Once the economy slumped, the military's days in office were numbered. The Latin American debt crisis of 1982 (*see* p. 72) saw foreign investment and loans stop and interest rates and prices rise sharply. Civilian presidents of the 1980s and 1990s tried to tackle inflation with different degrees of success.

The Death of Neves

Brazil's return to democracy was blighted by tragedy. The first civilian-elected leader in 22 years, Tancredo Neves, was a moderate, opposed to the military and acceptable to both conservative and liberal wings of political opinion. The night before he was to be sworn in as president, he fell ill. A month later he died and Brazil was plunged into a new crisis. Neves' deputy, José Sarney, was sworn in as the acting president in March 1985.

Sarney's term in office was doomed to failure because of the worsening economic situation. At the start of 1986, inflation rose to 330 percent. Sarney's economic Cruzado Plan led to a temporary boom but, once inflation started to rise again, Sarney lost popularity, although he stayed in power until March 1990.

The Debt Crisis

Rising profits from oil for Venezuela and Mexico and strong economic growth in the rest of South America in the 1970s led countries in the region to increase their level of borrowing. Western banks pressured the South American governments to take on more debt, fueling an already precarious situation. Latin America's foreign debt increased tenfold from 1970 to 1980. The world recession after 1980 and increased interest rates in the U.S. and Europe to curb inflation led to higher interest payments for the South American economies and a debt burden that soon spiraled out of control. The result was a grave economic situation for Latin America during the 1980s, with negative economic growth, spending cuts on public services, and large price increases.

Collor and Corruption

Sarney's successor was a flamboyant, young, and largely unknown former governor of the northeastern state of Alagoas, Fernando Collor de Mello. Collor's main opponent in the elections of November 1989 was the workers' leader Lula (see p. 71), now leader of the Worker's Party and a respected nationalist politician. Collor temporarily succeeded in stopping the runaway inflation but he never completed his term. Halfway through his presidency, he was suspended from office after the Brazilian Congress voted to impeach him on charges of corruption. Denounced by his own brother, it turned out that Collor stood at the center of a web of corruption mastermined by the treasury minister, Farias, who had effectively set up a parallel government, skimming off billions of dollars of public money into private schemes and bank accounts. Collor avoided impeachment by resigning on December 29, 1992, moving into exile in Miami. His vice-president, Itamar Franco, took over and had little success in tackling inflation and poverty until his finance minister, Fernando Henrique Cardoso, introduced the Real Plan.

Fernando Henrique Cardoso

Cardoso's success in introducing a new currency, the real, equivalent to the U.S. dollar, led to him being elected the next president. Cardoso represented an alliance of three parties: the Brazilian Social Democrat Party (PSDB), the Liberal Front (PFL), and the Labor Party (PTB). The alliance failed to win an overall majority in either house of parliament. Cardoso's lack of a majority enabled the opposition to block some of his changes and he was unable to reform the tax and social welfare system.

The Currency Crisis

Cardoso's popularity and his election to a second term in October 1998 stemmed from his successful control of the Brazilian economy. The success was threatened by the collapse of many Southeast Asian economies in 1997. After Russia defaulted on its debt, international financial speculators put intense pressure on the Brazilian real. As a result, interest rates in Brazil were raised by 50 percent and $30 billion in foreign capital left the country in August and September 1998. The International Monetary Fund forged Brazil a $41.5 billion aid program in November 1998. In January 1999, the Real Plan was abandoned, the currency was devalued by 8 percent, and the real became a free-floating currency, no longer tied to the dollar.

In June 1992, Rio hosted the Earth Summit. This was a meeting of 114 heads of government formed to discuss environmental issues. The Rio Declaration outlined 27 principles supporting sustainable development of environmental resources. The summit did much to focus attention on the plight of the Amazon region.

The Political Future

Despite the fall in the value of the Brazilian real, austerity measures announced as a result, and banking scandals that emerged in 1999, Cardoso was the president chosen to see Brazil into the 21st century. A series of amendments to the constitution has reinforced democracy and a return to military rule looks ever less likely. The main problem that faces the president and Brazil is the one that has dogged its history: social inequality, which affects every aspect of Brazilian life from employment and housing to education and welfare. The opposition has suggested that only by separating itself from the interests of big business can the government hope to achieve these aims

POLITICAL ORGANIZATION

Brazil is a presidential republic like the United States. The president is both the chief of state and the head of the government. Brazil is divided into one federal district and 26 states, each with an elected governor and regional parliament. A new constitution in 1988 set out the president's powers to choose his ministers of state, initiate legislation, and maintain foreign relations. The president is also commander-in-chief of the armed forces and has the power of total veto. The president is elected for a four-year term. To balance the president's power, the government is made up of an 81-seat

Presidents of Brazil since 1914:
- H. Rodrigues da Fonseca (1910–1914)
- V. Brás Pereira Gomes (1914–1918)
- F. de Paula Rodrigues Alves (1918–1919)
- E. Pessoa (1919–1922)
- A. da Silva Bernardes (1922–1926)
- W. Luis Pereira de Sousa (1926–1930)
- G. Vargas (1930–1945)
- E. Gaspar Dutra (1945–1950)
- G. Vargas (1950–1954)

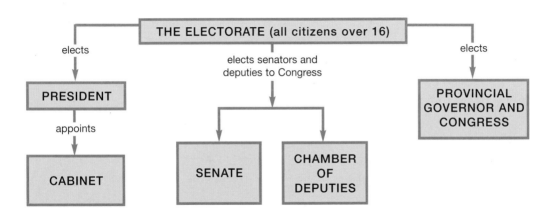

THE ELECTORATE (all citizens over 16)

elects → PRESIDENT → appoints → CABINET

elects senators and deputies to Congress → SENATE / CHAMBER OF DEPUTIES

elects → PROVINCIAL GOVERNOR AND CONGRESS

THE NATIONAL CONGRESS IN 2000

President: Fernando Henrique Cardoso • President is elected for a four-year term

Federal Senate
81 members elected for an eight-year term • One-third of seats reelected every four years

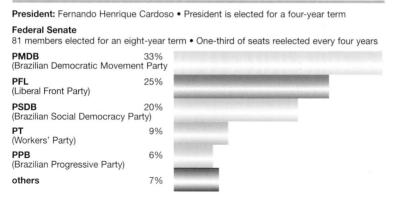

PMDB (Brazilian Democratic Movement Party	33%
PFL (Liberal Front Party)	25%
PSDB (Brazilian Social Democracy Party)	20%
PT (Workers' Party)	9%
PPB (Brazilian Progressive Party)	6%
others	7%

Chamber of Deputies
513 members • Last election 1998 • Members elected for a four-year term

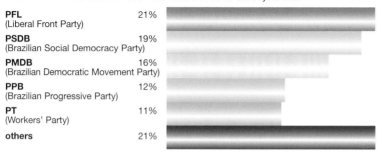

PFL (Liberal Front Party)	21%
PSDB (Brazilian Social Democracy Party)	19%
PMDB (Brazilian Democratic Movement Party)	16%
PPB (Brazilian Progressive Party)	12%
PT (Workers' Party)	11%
others	21%

Federal Senate and a 513-seat Chamber of Deputies. Members of the Senate are elected for eight-year terms and a third of the seats come up for reelection every four years. The Chamber of Deputies is reelected every four years by the system of proportional representation, which means that the percentage of seats for each party in the chamber is equal to its received percentage of the vote. Elections for both chambers occur on the same day. Legislation goes before both chambers of Congress and can take years to be approved. The number of political parties changes. In 1998, at the last elections, there were 18.

The current governing coalition is made up of four parties, the PSDB, the PMDB, the PFL, and the PPB. Opposition is provided by the Landless Workers' Movement, the labor unions, the Workers' Party, and the left-wing of the Catholic church.

Presidents of Brazil (cont.):
• Café Filho (1954–1955)
• C. Combra da Luz (1955)
• N. de Oliveira Ramos (1955–1956)
• J. Kubitschek (1956–1961)
• J. Quadros (1961)
• J. Goulart (1961–1963)
• P. Mazilli (1963)
• J. Goulart (1963–1964)
• P. Mazilli (1964)
• H. de Alencar Castelo Branco (1964–1967)
• A. da Costa e Silva (1967–1969)
• E. Médici (1969–1974)
• E. Geisel (1974–1979)
• J. de Oliveira Figueiredo (1979–1985)
• J. Sarney (1985–1990)
• F. Collor de Mello (1990-1992)
• Itamar Franco (1992–1994)
• F. Cardoso (1994–)

The Economy

"The economy is doing fine, but the people aren't."

Former Brazilian head of state General Emilio Medici in 1971

By the end of the 20th century Brazil's economy was the largest in South America and the eighth largest in the world. With its vast natural resources of minerals and agricultural products, Brazil always had the potential to become one of the world's great economies, but its history has been marked by booms followed by depressions that have left it vulnerable to economic stagnation and a failure to achieve its promise. Hyperinflation (massive rises in the price of goods) blighted the economy for much of the late-20th century.

A succession of natural resources (rubber, gold, coffee, and sugar) drew masses of immigrants to the country and produced a series of "booms" that fired the Brazilian economy. Brazil was an agricultural economy until the 20th century, when industrialization took over. Poorer Brazilians often left the countryside for the expanding cities because of a lack of land.

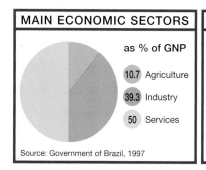

MAIN ECONOMIC SECTORS

as % of GNP

10.7 Agriculture

39.3 Industry

50 Services

Source: Government of Brazil, 1997

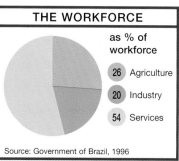

THE WORKFORCE

as % of workforce

26 Agriculture

20 Industry

54 Services

Source: Government of Brazil, 1996

Brazilian coffee farmers produce nearly twice as much coffee as their nearest rivals—those in Colombia. Coffee is Brazil's fourth-largest export.

MAIN ECONOMIC SECTORS

From the 1930s to 1950s government planning and investment in new technology and industry led to the rapid industrialization of the economy. During the 1960s and 1970s Brazil's GDP grew by a remarkable 11 percent a year. More recently, the development of new technology such as computing and the expansion of the banking sector have led to the urbanization of the Brazilian workforce.

Farming

"Everything that is planted here, grows," wrote Pedro Cabral, the Portuguese explorer who landed in Brazil in 1500. For most of the next 500 years Brazil continued to be an agriculture-based economy. At different times Brazilian raw products such as sugar, coffee, and rubber have dominated world trade. The exploitation of Brazil's raw materials started with the original Portuguese discoverers, who exported brazil wood until supplies were virtually exhausted.

Today, agriculture accounts for just under 11 percent of Brazil's total GDP. Despite this small proportion, the actual figures for agricultural production are impressive. In 1997, Brazil exported more than $5.6 billion of agricultural produce, making it one of the world's major agricultural producers: first in coffee production, second in both sugar and fruit, third for meat, fourth for cocoa, fifth for coarse grains, eighth for cotton, and tenth for rice. The diversity of Brazil's exports is one of its great strengths.

The northwest of the country is dominated by the Amazonian rain forest, while cropland is concentrated along the east coast. Cattle farming is a major industry in the center of the country.

HOW BRAZIL USES ITS LAND

Cropland

Forest

Pasture

Sugar

Sugar farming was introduced to northeast Brazil in 1532. In the second half of the 1600s and throughout the entire 17th century, the provinces of Bahia, Pernambuco, and Paraíba were the prime sources of sugar. Sugar is grown on plantations that, before mechanization, required a huge total labor force. People from Africa were enslaved and then transported to work the plantations. During the colonial period, sugar produced over half of all the export earnings. Today, most of the sugarcane grown is used to produce alcohol fuel for cars. At its peak in the 1980s, alcohol fuel provided over 10 percent of Brazil's total energy needs. It still powers millions of cars; 22 percent alcohol is added to gasoline.

The sugar plantations of northeastern Brazil are no longer the force in the economy that they once were. Labor there is hard and many prefer to move to the big cities to seek other employment.

Coffee

Like sugar, coffee was introduced to Brazil from abroad. By the 1900s Brazil had grown into the world's chief coffee exporter and coffee

LAND USE

%

6 Arable land

22 Permanent pasture

58 Forests/woodland

14 Other uses

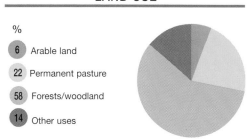

Source: Government of Brazil, 1993 (est.)

MAIN TRADING PARTNERS

EXPORTS

%

17.8	United States
12.8	Argentina
7.5	Netherlands
5.8	Japan
56.1	Others

IMPORTS

%

23.4	United States
13.4	Argentina
8.4	Germany
5.9	Japan
48.9	Others

Source: *Economist World in Figures, 2000*

remained Brazil's leading export until 1973. Immigrants flocked to Brazil at the end of the 19th century (nearly one million between 1879 and 1890 alone) to work on coffee plantations. Most settled in São Paulo state, transforming São Paulo itself from a provincial town into Brazil's main financial center.

Unlike sugar, coffee helped to spread wealth. It could be grown by smallholders and it was not the only crop grown at one time. Often, coffee growers would grow beans and cereals between the rows of coffee plants. Coffee also encouraged other types of economic development, such as railroads and ports, which were built to transport the coffee beans across Brazil and overseas. Coffee continues to be a major Brazilian export.

Rubber

The rubber boom was the shortest of all the agricultural booms (*see* p. 65). It started in the 1890s as a result of the United States' and Europe's insatiable demand for rubber, needed for tires for bicycles and automobiles. When rubber seeds were smuggled out of Brazil and successfully grown in British eastern colonies, such as Malaysia and India, the rubber trade collapsed and Brazil's rubber share fell from 90 percent of the world market in 1910 to 2 percent in 1937. Fortunately this period coincided with the country's rapid industrialization.

EXPORTS ($bn)	
● Manufactured goods	32.7
● Transport equipment	6.8
● Soybeans	5.7
● Iron ore	4.9
● Coffee	3.1
Total (including others)	53

Source: *Economist World in Figures, 2000*

IMPORTS ($bn)	
● Machinery & electrical equipment	19.8
● Fuels and lubricants	8.9
● Transport equipment & parts	6.5
● Chemical products	3.3
Total (including others)	61.4

Land Reform

Despite Brazil's rich agricultural land and vast tracts of uncultivated but potentially farmable land, poverty and homelessness is a problem for five million Brazilian families. This is because 10 percent of the farmers own 80 percent of the land. Land reform is badly needed in Brazil to redistribute wealth more evenly. Every government since 1964 has promised land reform, but it is always blocked by a combination of powerful landowners and the complicated bureaucracy of Brazil's Congress.

Sem Terra Movement

The Landless Movement (*Sem Terra* Movement or MST) was started in 1984 by a group of rural activists who decided that land reform would only happen with direct action. Under the slogan "Occupy, Resist, and Produce," the activists began seizing large, unused estates across Brazil. In Brazilian law, any unproductive land can be seized. The activists chose each estate carefully so that their occupation was not illegal. Since it started, the landless movement has settled more than 131,000 families and reclaimed over 22 million acres of land. The movement faces much opposition and in the first three years of the Cardoso government (1994–1996) there were two massacres of *Sem Terra* activists.

Fishing

Despite having a coastline of more than 4,500 miles (7,491 km), Brazil is not a major exporter of fish. However, fish is a major foodstuff for people living along the coast. Along the Amazon River there is a large freshwater catch, which forms the basis of Amazonian cuisine.

Mineral Wealth

Brazil is extremely rich in both metals and minerals. It has one-third of the world's known iron ore reserves and it also exports manganese, tin, and copper. Diamonds are found in Brazil and they, too, attracted a rush after their discovery in 1729. The metal that made much of Brazil's wealth was gold.

Brazil lacks one important natural resource: oil. Many of its economic problems of the 1970s and 1980s stemmed from rises in international oil prices, which sent its foreign debt even higher. The oil industry was brought under state control in 1953 but in 1995 the

ENERGY SOURCES

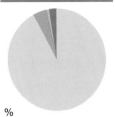

%

92.1 Hydroelectric power

4.4 Fossil fuels (coal, gas, oil)

0.8 Nuclear

2.7 Other

Source: *CIA World Fact Book, 1996*

The Gold Rush

Gold was first discovered in 1695 in the state of Minas Gerais (whose name translates as "General Mines"). This transformed the state from a wilderness into a well-populated region. The mines had the largest deposits of gold in the western hemisphere and news of them spread fast. The gold rush lasted 100 years, during which period Brazil had the highest per capita income in the world. Fortunes were made and settlements such as Ouro Prêto (Black Gold) grew from small hamlets to large towns.

Gold is still mined today, both in closed and open mines, where the gold is found on the surface. In the 1980s the open mine Serra Pelada ("Naked Mountain," above), attracted 80,000 *garimpeiros* (wildcat gold miners) who rushed to mine the gold, digging it from the surface with their bare hands. A couple of them made fortunes, but many lost their lives. The area has now been closed for environmental recuperation. In 1996, a large gold mine was discovered which is expected to produce ten tons of gold a year, 20 percent of Brazil's annual output.

Brazilian Congress voted to allow competition in an effort to make it more efficient. In a further effort to lessen its dependency on imported oil, Brazil has developed alcohol fuel. Hydroelectricity has been produced by building dams such as that at Itaipu, owned jointly with Paraguay. The dam has the capacity to supply all the electricity needs of Paraguay and southern Brazil.

Industry

Brazil's industrial output makes up nearly 40 percent of the country's total production yet industrialization only happened in the last half of the 20th century. Brazil's industrial effort was started by the creation of giant state industries out of steel and oil companies controlled by the government, and by improving the railroads.

The decision by the government to invest in industry led to rapid urbanization and foreign investment.

Computers
Electronics
Coffee
Timber
Automobile assembly
Sugar
Banking and finance

MAJOR INDUSTRIES

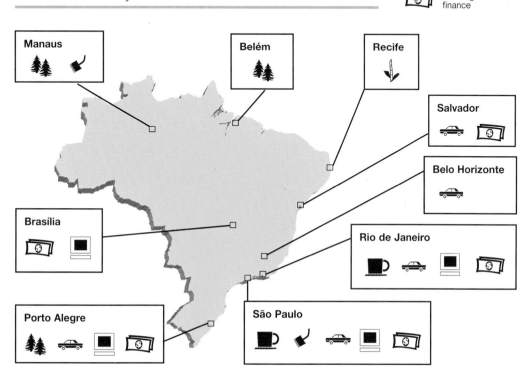

Manaus

Belém

Recife

Salvador

Belo Horizonte

Brasília

Rio de Janeiro

Porto Alegre

São Paulo

Brazil's automobile industry was set up by the government in the 1950s to replace imports from Germany and the United States. It is one of the success stories of the Brazilian economy.

Poorer people from all over Brazil flocked to São Paulo and the surrounding area to work in the factories set up by U.S. and European companies. Companies were attracted to Brazil because of lower taxes offered to them as an incentive by the government. Today key industries are the manufacturing of textiles, shoes, chemicals, cement, metals such as iron and steel, aircraft, motor vehicles and parts, and other machinery and equipment. Some 20 percent of the workforce is employed in Brazil's various industries, compared to over 26 percent of the workforce in agriculture.

Brazilian industry has become increasingly efficient with the privatization of previously state-owned industries, the abolition of price controls, and falling prices. Companies are facing competition for the first time, which has led them to modernize equipment and working practices.

Services

Service industries are those that do not produce anything, like manufacturing, but provide support, such as finance, for the rest of the economy. Services make up the largest part of the Brazilian economy. They generated 50 percent of the country's income in 1997 and employed 54 percent of the workforce. Since the introduction of the Real Plan (*see* box, opposite), Brazil has attracted more financial investment from overseas; bankers fly in from all over the world to São Paulo. The potential for economic growth is strong, but Brazil's chief economic problem remains the inequality in wealth distribution.

Despite this, Brazilian unemployment is low, at around 6.9 percent. One of the reasons for this is that an entire

The Real Plan

By 1993 Brazil's inflation (the annual rate of price increases) had reached 2,708 percent. This means that goods at the end of the year were over 27 times as expensive as at the beginning. In 1994, Fernando Cardoso, then the finance minister, devised a plan to control inflation and to allow for Brazil to plan financially.

He replaced the existing currency, the cruzeiro, with the real and fixed the exchange rate at equal to one U.S. dollar. The result of introducing a stable currency (one that did not change in value) was a reduction in inflation that allowed Brazilians to spend without fears for the future. This improved the economy and attracted overseas investment. In 1997 the United States alone invested $16 billion.

Along with Argentina, Paraguay, and Uruguay, Brazil is a member of the Southern Cone Trading Partnership, known as MERCOSUL in Portuguese (see map). Members of MERCOSUL trade without charging one another the duties that are usually paid by trading countries. Since MERCOSUL started in 1991, Brazil and Argentina have tripled the business they do with each other.

The Real Plan stabilized Brazil's economy but the country was rocked by the Asian financial crisis in fall 1997 (see p. 73). Brazil managed to avoid the shock waves of the crisis by devaluing its currency by 40 percent in January 1999.

Members of MERCOSUL

Associate members of MERCOSUL

Non-members of MERCOSUL

The South American trading bloc MERCOSUL appears ready to expand in the 21st century. Two other Latin American countries—Chile and Bolivia—have become associate (part) members of the bloc.

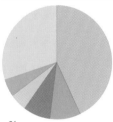

%

43	Argentina
9	Uruguay
8	United States
5	Paraguay
5	Germany
30	Other

Source: Government of Brazil, 1997

industry has been created by an underclass that is employed by the middle classes. Cheap labor is plentiful in Brazil. It is not unusual for a middle-class family to hire two or more live-in maids and other servants, usually from the *favelas*, to walk their dogs, or deliver groceries.

Tourism

A service industry that is still underdeveloped is tourism. In 1997, some 2.8 million tourists visited Brazil and spent $972 million, compared to 48.4 million tourist arrivals in the U.S. and revenues of $70 billion. Many tourists think of Brazil only as a place to visit at Carnival time or to see the Amazon rain forest. However, this vast country has much more to offer. Among its top attractions are thousands of miles of sandy beaches, interesting colonial towns to explore, wildlife reserves, and outstanding natural beauty. Much could be done to expand Brazil's tourism and to bring investment to poor areas, particularly the northeast. The main problem at the moment is a lack of low-cost air fares since aviation is controlled by the air force. There are also relatively few tourist services.

Tourist schooners anchor in the harbor at Ilhados Frades during their daily excursion to Itaparica in Bahia.

COMMUNICATIONS AND TRANSPORT

Brazil's size means that the distances to be covered are very large and that major cities are far from each other. For example, Brasília is 596 miles (960 km) from Rio.

TRANSPORTATION

The Transamazônica Highway and the roads connecting Brasília and the northeast coast, all projects completed since the 1960s, stand out on the transportation map of Brazil. Traditionally Brazil's transportation network has served the Atlantic coastline and there is a well-developed system in the industrialized southeast. The major method of transportation in Amazonia is the Amazon River itself, which has served as a route for thousands of years. Development of the Brazilian interior has proved sporadic, with mountainous terrain, rain forest, and regional underdevelopment as perennial barriers.

The main means of transportation in Brazil is by road. Most Brazilians do not have automobiles, however, and use long-distance buses to travel from city to city. There is an extensive air network throughout Brazil, but the average Brazilian cannot afford the high fares. Brazil's railroad network is very small.

Legend:
- —— Major highways
- ┼┼┼┼ Railroad
- ✈ Major airport
- —— Navigable river

Highways and Roads

Brazil has 1,204,871 miles (1,939 million km) of highways of which less than 10 percent are paved. Brazilian buses, the major form of transport, travel all over the country on paved and unpaved roads. The coastal highways are in good condition but outside of the major

Brazil's Longest Bus Jouney

Brazil's longest bus journey starts in Cascavel in the state of Paraná in southern Brazil on the Argentine border and ends in Santa Helena in Venezuela. The passengers travel from the vast pampas to the Caribbean, a distance of 3,000 miles (5,000 km). It is like traveling from Los Angeles to St. Louis and back. The journey takes one week, with lots of stops on the way.

population areas road quality is much worse. In Amazonia and the *sertão* region the roads often alternate between dirt tracks and pot-hole-filled tarmac roads, preventing any smooth flow of traffic.

Brazilians have a saying: "Progress is roads." During the military dictatorships of the 1960s many road-building projects were undertaken. The best known, the Transamazônica Highway, was intended as a link between the Amazon region and the rest of Brazil and South America. It was almost 3,500 miles (5,400 km) long, stretching from the Peruvian border through Brazil to the Atlantic Ocean. The military government wanted to relocate landless peasants from the northeast to the Amazon basin, but the project failed despite huge financial investment. Today the road has deteriorated and only parts of it are open to traffic. Other road projects in the Amazon

Roadbuilding in the Amazon region (below) has been controversial. It leads to the destruction of unique habitats, but has proved crucial to the local economy.

region have suffered a similar fate and remain unused because settlers have failed to arrive in Amazonia in sufficiently large numbers.

Buses are a way of life in Brazil. They vary from the top-rated *leito* (sleeper) buses, which have fully reclining seats with blankets, pillows, and a steward service, to the *comum* (ordinary) bus. On busy routes such as the six-hour journey between Rio de Janeiro and São Paulo, buses depart every 15 minutes. On other routes, such as the Rio-Belém route, which takes 52 hours, there is one bus a day. Buses make frequent stops on long journeys at *rodoviárias* (bus stations) where passengers can buy food and drink and use the restroom (although most buses have a restroom on board).

Passengers wait for a bus at São Paulo bus station. Bus transport is often crowded and people use the buses to transport large amounts of luggage and produce.

Buses are operated by hundreds of private companies, but prices are standardized, even where two companies compete for the same route. Local bus services operate to the smaller, more isolated towns. These buses are quite different from the intercity buses, which generally leave from the outskirts of town. Often overcrowded, local buses stop everywhere to pick up people who are usually traveling with large parcels for the market and sometimes with animals. It costs the same to travel whether you are able to get a seat or not.

City buses are usually crowded with commuters, particularly during rush hours. Despite this, fares are cheap and there is generally a flat rate.

Paranaguá Rail Trip

Every morning at 8:30 A.M. a train leaves the city of Curitiba for the 66-mile (110-km) journey to the southern seaport of Paranaguá. The train winds down toward the coast, clinging to the sides of the mountains. It crosses viaducts and passes through tunnels as it descends through the breathtaking scenery of Brazil's Atlantic rain forest, a lush, tropical vegetation broken up by waterfalls. The journey lasts three hours because the route to Paranaguá is so circuitous.

Rail Transportation

Apart from the crowded urban commuter lines, trains do not form an important part of Brazil's transportation network. There are over 17,000 miles (27,418 km) of track, of which just over 1,000 miles (1,750 km) are electrified. Trains are used mainly to transport cargo. For the tourist, there are a number of scenic rail journeys through the heart of Brazil (*see* box).

River and Sea

With its long coastline, Brazil has many seaports and harbors. These include Belém, Fortaleza, Itabuna, Paranaguá, Pôrto Alegre, Recife, Rio de Janeiro, Rio Grande, Salvador, Santos, and Vitória.

Brazil also has river ports such as Manaus in the Amazon region. There, transportation by river is easier than by road, since so little of the land has been cleared. Both goods and people are frequently transported by river. Tourists can travel up the river and get a unique view of Amazonian life from the water. Travel is by *gaiola* (riverboat). The *gaiolas* provide a cheap and practical way of sailing along the Amazon River and its tributaries. Local residents and tourists alike string up hammocks on deck to sleep while the slow-moving boats travel through the humid climate. More passengers can travel on the *gaiola* in hammocks than in conventional cabins. The trip from Manaus, halfway along the Amazon, to Belém at the river's mouth takes just over a week.

In addition to the Amazonian river boats, there are also important ferry services serving the bays of Salvador and Rio de Janeiro and their surrounding areas.

The small city of Santarém, today with a population of about 120,000, stands on what was once the most populated area in the Amazon. The surrounding region has provided evidence of early rivercraft that traded along the settlements of the great Amazon River.

Air Travel

Brazil's air transport network is very extensive but too expensive for most Brazilians, who are more likely to rely on the intercity bus service. Five major airlines operate the domestic air routes. These are the national carrier, Varig, VASP, Transbrasil, RioSul, and TAM. For tourists, air travel is often the most practical way of covering large distances quickly and each airline offers heavily discounted air passes for foreign travelers. In addition to the commercial airlines, air taxis operate in the Amazon region and military planes also carry civilian passengers. Like the buses, planes between the north and south of Brazil often stop to pick up other passengers, sometimes in a relatively unscheduled way. A plane may stop up to four times between the two extremes of the country.

Brazil has almost 3,000 airports, of which 1,658 have paved runways and 1,213 unpaved runways. The major international airports are Santos Dumont in Rio de Janeiro and Guarulhos in São Paulo. Outside the major cities the airports are tiny, often with only one flight a day on a small propeller plane. In many areas, however, air transport is crucial for the movement of goods, so isolated communities are often dependent on these smaller aircraft.

The gaiolas provide the only means of public transportation on the narrower stretches of the Amazon River's tributaries.

Arts and Living

"Power lies in the growth of awareness."

Brazilian human rights activist Herbert de Souza

Brazil's cultural history is very different from that of the Spanish-speaking countries of Latin America. When the Portuguese arrived in 1500, Brazil did not have a highly organized and developed civilization as existed in neighboring Inca Peru and parts of Central America and Mexico. At that time, Brazil was inhabited by the Tupí-Guaraní native people who, because of Brazil's tropical climate and their nomadic lifestyle, lived in temporary settlements in dwellings made from branches, leaves, and vegetable fibers. Much of this early culture has been lost because of its temporary nature.

The printed word came late to Brazil. The first printing press arrived with the Portuguese king Dom João VI in 1808. Many Brazilians do not have sufficient literacy to read a newspaper or magazine, so television, film, and radio provide their means of relaxation and information, although there are many Brazilian writers and Brazilians are buying more books than ever. Books are often sold in partworks, magazine-length sections sold with newspapers or periodicals.

The biggest event in Brazil's calendar is Carnival, a five-day street party held each year before the start of Lent in the Christian calendar. Carnival celebrates Brazil's love of music and dance. The flamboyance and extravagance of Carnival captures the spirit of Brazilian culture.

Elements from colonial street celebrations, 19th-century masquerade balls, and 20th-century samba combined to create today's Carnival procession.

THE ARTS

In the early 20th century Brazilian artists looked to international movements such as Modernism to free them from the legacy of colonialism. In the last 50 years, as the country's confidence has grown, Brazil has more fully appreciated its unique qualities. In painting this has meant developing a palette influenced by the vibrancy of daily life. Literature has begun to examine the social problems that underlie Brazilian society, but it is perhaps in music that Brazil has developed its most powerful national voice, one that is now heard the world over.

A young man from the Palaxo tribe paints the face of his brother at Coroa Vermelha in Bahia state, where nearly 2,500 Indians were meeting for the 2000 Brazilian Indians' Congress.

Painting and sculpture

Brazilian art is derived from many different influences. In the 20th century it has been at the forefront of Brazil's attempts to find a distinctive identity.

In 1922, *Semana da Arte Moderne* (Modern Art

Oscar Niemeyer's space-age Museum of Contemporary Art stands across the bay from Rio at Niterói. It was completed in 1997.

Week) was held in São Paulo to commemorate 100 years of independence. The week-long event captured a mood that artists and writers had felt for several years: that the future lay not with Europe and its influences, but at home in Brazil. Painters of the day, such as Cândido Portinari (1903–1962), used huge murals to expose the exploitation and injustice of life suffered by Brazil's coffee plantation workers and miners.

As the century went on, the artistic communities of Rio and São Paulo developed a healthy rivalry as both movements worked to establish Brazil's reputation for modern abstract art on the international stage. The repression of the military dictatorships led artists to disguise their subject matter and ironically led to an enrichment of their art as they searched for more elaborate ways to express their ideas. In 1970 Antônio Enrique Amaral (born 1935) used the banana as his subject. In a series of paintings he portrayed the banana as a symbol of power and fruitfulness, an ironic response to Latin

Song of the Exile

There are palm trees in my country.
And the singing Sabiá;
The birds warbling here
Don't sing as they do there.

Our heavens have more stars,
Our meadows far more blooms,
Our forests have more life,
Our life has much more love.

When I dream, alone, at night,
I find more pleasures there;
There are palm trees in my country
And the singing Sabiá.

My country has a loveliness
That I don't find here;
When I dream—alone at night—
I find more pleasures there;
There are palm trees in my country,
And the singing Sabiá.

May God not let me perish
Without going back there;
Without knowing the loveliness
I cannot find here;
Without a glimpse of palm trees
And the singing Sabiá.

America's dismissal by the developed world as "banana republics." At the end of the 20th century Brazilian conceptual art—art based on an abstract idea—continued to flourish while remaining largely unknown to the outside world.

Literature

Colonial literature consisted mostly of plays and poetry. The first plays to be staged in the 16th century were religious in nature and were performed in three languages: Portuguese, Spanish, and Tupí. With the arrival of the Portuguese court in Rio de Janeiro in 1808, 19th-century Brazilian literature became heavily influenced by Europe. Every European literary movement (Romanticism, Realism, and Symbolism) had a Brazilian following, with attempts made to adapt the different literary styles to local interests.

In the middle of the 19th century "the native" became the focus of Brazil's Romantic writers, who idealized the native population and ignored the brutal treatment they suffered. The two most famous writers of this period were Antônio Gonçalves Dias (1823–1864), a poet who expressed a nostalgia for Brazil as a tropical Eden, and the novelist José de Alencar (1829–1877), who attempted to describe Brazil in all its complexity. Gonçalves Dias wrote Brazil's most famous poem *"Canção do exílio"* ("Song of the Exile", *see* box), which is still recited today.

Brazilian Novels

Joaquim Maria Machado de Assis (1839–1908) is considered by many to be Brazil's greatest author. Machado's life-story is one of rags-to-riches. Born the son of a freed slave, he ended his life as an establishment figure, father of the Brazilian Academy of Letters. He wrote nine novels and more than 200 short stories, as well as poetry and journalism. His work evaluated and reflected Brazilian society, and dealt particularly with slavery, which was abolished during his lifetime in 1888.

20th-Century Literature

In the 1920s writers became increasingly concerned with national identity. They wanted to portray the real Brazil and release it from what they saw as stereotypes. Poetry, particularly the work of Manuel Bandeira (1886–1968) and Carlos Drummond de Andrade (1902–1987), was most successful at capturing the ethos of Brazil.

The French anthropologist Claude Lévi-Strauss wrote a study of his four-year stay in Brazil in the 1930s entitled *Tristes Tropiques (Sad Tropics)*. He describes his time with the Nambikwara and Tupi–Kawahib Indians and the rise of São Paulo as a major city.

Brazil's Most Famous Book

If Machado is Brazil's most famous writer, then *Os sertões* by Euclides da Cunha (1866–1909) is arguably Brazil's most famous book. It tells the true story of Antônio Conselheiro, a lay preacher who wandered the *sertão* between 1871 and 1893 and helped people by reconstructing abandoned churches and chapels and building roads and dams. Local landowners and priests supported him and relied on his large bands of workers. However, in 1893 he got caught up in local political rivalries after he led a demonstration against the newly formed Republic of Brazil. He and his followers fled to Canudos, an abandoned ranch in the state of Bahia. Canudos grew into one of the largest towns in the northeast, with almost 30,000 inhabitants in search of a better life. The central government considered Conselheiro a threat to their power and in January 1897 troops went to Canudos to destroy the community and kill Conselheiro. Canudos was dynamited and burned to the ground with huge loss of life on both sides. The campaign was considered a failure because victory only came with the deaths of 5,000 soldiers and 20,000 *sertânistas*. Euclides used the campaign to criticize a social system that excluded most people.

Elizabeth Bishop (1911–1979)

Regarded as one of North America's finest poets, Elizabeth Bishop made her home in Brazil between 1952 and 1967 and wrote many of her best-known poems there. She lived in Rio de Janeiro, Petrópolis, and later in the colonial town of Ouro Prêto. Her poems reflected daily life in the Rio slums. Brazilians were proud of their adopted daughter and awarded her many prizes for her writing.

In the 1930s literature reached wider audiences as Brazil became increasingly urbanized. Initially, literature had shown a rural bias but it then started to play its part in reducing the gaps between social groups. Jorge Amado (born 1912), the most popular Brazilian writer of the 20th century both in Brazil and abroad, set his novels in the countryside and the city. The 1940s and 1950s saw novels become more experimental and adventurous. Amado's 1958 novel *Gabriela, cravo e canela* (*Gabriela, Clove, and Cinnamon*) was hugely popular, selling 100,000 copies in its first year.

There have been few famous women Brazilian writers. One exception was Clarice Lispector (1920–1977) who found an audience outside Brazil as well as at home. Her stories are usually set in Rio and have women as their main characters. Other popular women writers did not write novels. Instead, their personal diaries were published to wide acclaim. Helena Morley's *Minha vida de menina*, only published in 1942, is a teenager's diary of life in Diamantina, a mining town in Minas Gerais, at the end of the 19th century. The American poet Elizabeth Bishop translated it into English as *The Diary of Helena Morley*.

The military dictatorship of the 1960s led to a profound change in the country's literature because writers had to contend with censorship and the increasing use of torture as the military sought to repress their political enemies. At the same time, Brazil was changing rapidly as industrialization gathered speed and immigrants arrived to work in the newly opened factories. Protest literature appeared for the first time as writing became increasingly politicized. At the end of the 20th century satirical novels were published which examined the social inequities so prevalent in Brazil.

Movies

Brazilians love to go to the movies. Despite having one of the world's largest movie audiences, however, the Brazilian film industry has never established itself as a leading power. In the 1960s the *Cinema Nôvo* (New Cinema) won critical acclaim with movies that mixed social realism and religion, but military censorship prevented the industry from expanding further.

During the 1970s and 1980s political films were banned. Brazil produced mainly children's movies and imported and subtitled Hollywood movies. In the late 1990s the Brazilian film industry showed signs of a revival with movies such as *Central Station*, which won a 1999 Academy Award for best foreign-language film.

Architecture

Brazil offers many different types of architecture, from colonial styles in towns such as Ouro Prêto and Salvador to the modernist vision of Oscar Niemeyer and Lúcio Costa in Brasília. For many architects Brasília was seen as an inspiration, being a completely new city that put into practice the theories of European architects such as Le Corbusier (1887–1965).

Brazil's buildings offer a striking contrast between hi-tech developments and the most basic shanty towns, such as here on the outskirts of São Paulo.

Curitiba

In Curitiba, in the southern state of Paraná, architecture and town planning have radically altered the city. Much of the change in the city is due to the work of one man, architect Jaime Lerner, who realized that to bring about vital changes needed for Curitiba, he would achieve more as a politician than as an architect. Serving for three terms as mayor from 1970 to 1990, Lerner introduced an efficient public transportation network, banned private cars from parts of the city, increased the number of public parks, and improved the conditions of the *favelas*. The result is that people are flocking to Curitiba because its quality of life is so much higher than that of other Brazilian cities. Economists calculated that workers in Curitiba spend on average an hour a day less to commute to work than workers in São Paulo.

Carmen Miranda

The height of samba's popularity was the 1930s and its most famous singer was the Portuguese-born Carmen Miranda (1909–1955), who moved to Rio while still a baby. Flamboyantly dressed, and famous for a headdress piled high with fruit, Miranda is remembered as the international ambassador of the samba. She became a singing star across Latin America in the 1930s before moving to Hollywood, where she starred in many movies, including such hit films as *That Night in Rio* (1941). At one point in the 1940s, Miranda was the highest-paid movie star in America before her career collapsed. Samba remains the most popular music in Brazil today; its popularity has spread to North America and Europe. The carnival in Rio de Janeiro is the biggest samba show in the world.

Music

Brazilians love music which, perhaps more than any other art form, reflects their multicultural heritage. Wherever you go, people are playing, singing, and dancing to their favorite songs. Music and dance are a celebration and a group activity, and are where Brazil's reputation for partying and enjoying life originates. Music is also a particularly important form of communication in a country where many people cannot read. TV and radio commercials are often sung, and during political elections each party has its own theme tune.

Carnival in Rio

Carnival (*Carnaval* in Portuguese) is a huge street party with samba parades as the main event. Rio's *escolas de samba* (samba clubs) begin rehearsals for the parade months beforehand. Each of the 16 major schools takes a different theme each year: usually an interpretation of a historical event or from current affairs. Each night during Carnival the parades begin at 7:00 P.M. and last up to 12 hours. Each samba school has up to 3,000 *sambistas*, including 400 drummers making an unbelievably loud noise. The parades consist of floats that tell the chosen story, using flamboyant costume, choreography, song, and of course, samba music. The judges take all these different components into consideration as they judge each school. Competition is fierce as every samba school is desperate to win.

For tourists and locals, Carnival is the chance to take part in a fantastic party while being entertained by the exotic and often outrageous displays of the samba schools. Nightly dances begin the month before Carnival officially starts, so once Carnival is over, Lent provides the exhausted revelers with a chance to catch up on their sleep.

A man puts the final touches to costumes for participants in the Rio Carnival.

Music in Brazil varies from region to region. In the south, near Argentina, *gauchos* (those from Rio Grande do Sul) sing along to accordion music much as their German ancestors did. Farther north, in Mato Grosso do Sul, the influence is from the Spanish-speaking Paraguayans; in the northeast it is the African-influenced rhythms of *baião*, *forró*, and *maracatu*. In the Amazon region you can hear Caribbean music. Brazil is also home to the samba, bossa nova, and tropicalismo, which are enjoyed not only in Brazil but also all over the world.

The Manguiera Samba School dancers at the Rio Carnival with their display representing the "fruits of Brazil."

Samba

Samba is probably the most famous music to come out of Brazil. It is certainly the most popular. The music of the African slaves is the biggest influence on samba. Afro-Brazilian music is both social and religious, and musicians use the same instruments for religious ceremonies and parties. The word samba is used for both the music and the dancing. There are many different forms of both.

Bossa Nova

Bossa nova loosely means "new thing" and refers to a style of music that introduced not only Brazil but also the rest of the world to a new way of playing instruments and singing. Unlike samba, which came from the poor Afro-Brazilian *favelas*, bossa nova was the music of the urban, university-educated middle class. It started in the 1950s and, just as with the *Cinema Nôvo* and the building of Brasília, signaled to the rest of the world

Brazil's individuality. The most famous bossa nova song, still known and played across the world, is "The Girl from Ipanema" ("*A Garota de Ipanema*"), which was composed by Antônio Carlos (Tom) Jobim and Vinícius de Moraes, one of Brazil's best known poets.

Since bossa nova arrived on the music scene there have been many different musical styles. Tropicalismo dominated the end of the 1960s. It mixed all the styles and traditions of Brazilian music, and popular artists such as Gilberto Gil still play it today. Musicians such as Chico Buarque mix traditional samba with modern music, while the famous Brazilian singer Milton Nascimento blends modern rock with Brazilian music and political lyrics. Brazilian rock bands such as Kid Abelha and Plebe Urbana are popular with Brazil's teenagers.

Media

Brazil's media is dominated by television. Five national networks and about 250 local stations bring television to practically every corner of the country. Only one network, which broadcasts educational programs, is government controlled. The privately owned network, Globo TV, is the fourth largest network in the world after ABC, NBC, and CBS, but produces more hours of television than any other TV network—some 4,420 hours of drama, comedy, music, and news per year. Television's dominance over other media such as newspapers is partly explained by the low levels of literacy in Brazil, but also by the nation's obsession with *telenovelas*.

Telenovelas

Telenovelas are often translated into English as "soap operas," but the translation is a little misleading. *Telenovelas* are TV series that air six nights a week, with a 50-minute episode per night and a normal series run of about eight months. *Telenovelas* can be funny, sad, or romantic, or sometimes all three. They can deal with historical events or modern-day themes. Some are even based on novels, such as those of Jorge Amado. What every *telenovela* has in common is that almost everybody, from the rich Rio housewife to the *favela*-dweller eking out an existence, watches them. *Telenovelas* bind Brazil together and people discuss them. One critic described *telenovelas* as "the great aspirin of Brazil."

In spite of having half of the total illiterate population in Latin America, Brazil produces a large number of newspapers. *The Folha de São Paulo* is considered the country's best, but every major city has its own local newspaper. In Rio, for example, in addition to the more traditional newspapers such as *Jornal do Brasil* and *Jornal do Commércio*, there is the sensationalist *O Povo*, which concentrates on lurid stories and pictures.

Environmentalists and local fishermen in the village of Jericoacoara in Ceará state (above) have resisted develop-ment. People live there without cars or electricity.

EVERYDAY LIFE

In a country as big as Brazil daily life varies greatly for the country's different inhabitants. Most Brazilians live in cities, and life in a busy city such as São Paulo could not be more different from the life of some of the Amazon peoples. The citizens of São Paulo belong to the 21st century and the Amazonian peoples live in a time that has barely changed over the centuries.

How to Say...

Alongside soccer, Carnival, and the samba, Portuguese, the official language of Brazil, is one of the unifying features of the country. Here are some helpful everyday expressions that you might like to learn:

Hi *Oi* (oy)

Hello Good morning *Bom dia* (bom-DEE-ya)

Good afternoon/night *Boa tarde/boa noite* (boh-AH tar-day/boh-AH NOY-tay)

See you later *Até logo* (AH-tay-low-go)

How's it going? *Tudo bem?* (TOO-doo-bem)

How are you? *Come vai?* (kom-eh-VYE)

Thank you *Obrigado* (to a male) (ob-rig-AH-doo)

Obrigada (to a female) (ob-rig-AH-dah)

You're welcome *De nada* (deh-NAH-da)

Yes *Sim* (seem)

No *Não* (NAH-un)

Sorry *Desculpa* (des-COOL-pah)

Excuse me *Com licença* (COM lee SENsah)

I understand *Entendo* (en-TEN-doo)

I don't understand *Não entendo* (NAH-un en-TEN-doo)

Do you speak English? *Você fala inglês?* (voSAY-FAHla in-GLAYS)

Fine *Bem* (BEM)

What is your name?

Como se chama? (COM-o seh CHAH-ma)

My name is *O meu nome é*

(O MAYoo-NOmay–ay)

Where...?. *Onde...?* (ON-day)

When...? *Quando...?* (KWON-do)

What...? *Que?* (KEH) –

Numbers:

One/a *Um/uma* (OOM/OO-ma)

Two *Dois/Duas* (DOYS/DOO-as)

Three *Tres* (TRAYSH)

Four *Quatro* (KWA-troo)

Five *Cinco* (SINK-oo)

Six *Seis* (SAY-ish)

Seven *Sete* (SAY-chee)

Eight *Oito* (OYtoo)

Nine *Nove* (NOH-vay)

Ten *Dez* (dee-YEZ)

Days of the week:

Monday *Segunda-feira* (or *segunda*) (zeg-OON-dah FAY-rah)

Tuesday *Terça-feira* (or *terça*) (TER-sa FAY-rah)

Wednesday *Quarta-feira* (or *quarto*) (KWAR-ta FAY-rah)

Thursday *Quinta-feira* (or *quinto*) (KWEEN-ta FAY-rah)

Friday *Sexta-feira* (or *sexta*) (SAYS-ta FAY-rah)

Saturday *Sábado* (SA-ba-doo)

Sunday *Domingo* (doe-MIN-goo)

ATTENDANCE AT SCHOOL

College and university	11%
High school	15%
Elementary	100%

The above figures for school attendance are provided by the Brazilian government and do not agree with the lower figures given by independent agencies.

Education

Education in Brazil depends on social class. By law, school is compulsory at elementary and junior high level (between ages seven and 14), but it is estimated that out of 13 million children three million do not go to school. They cannot afford to go, even though education is free, because they must work to eat. Public schools are underfunded and there are not enough desks or even schools for everybody. Teachers in the public schools are poorly paid, so there is always a shortage of people willing to train for a teaching career. For the children who go on to high school level (15 to 18 years) conditions are usually better.

Many Brazilians find the public schools so bad that they pay to send their children to private schools. This is reflected at university level. Almost all university students come from private schools. University education is free in Brazil and there are more than 870 higher education institutes, which cater to 1.5 million students.

Brazil spends the same proportion of its GDP on education as many developed European countries, but while primary education is underfunded, children of wealthy parents pay nothing for a university education.

Literacy

The Brazilian government claims an 80 percent literacy rate but many people dispute that it is so high. EDUCAR, the government's own department for adult education, claims that only 40 percent of Brazilians are able to read a newspaper. Since 1971 there has been an adult literacy campaign to try and improve the situation. In 1972 educational programs started on TV and radio stations. It is even possible to train as a kindergarten teacher using TV and radio courses.

President Cardoso recognized that Brazil could not advance if it did not educate its children so he spearheaded attempts to educate more of them. But the problem remains huge.

Health and Welfare

In Brazil, perhaps more than any other country, the wealthier you are the healthier you are. Anyone who can afford to pay for medical care in urban districts can rely on well-run hospitals and well-trained staff. In poor rural areas, the nearest doctor is often miles away. In a country where the majority of people live in poverty, Brazil has more plastic surgeons per capita than any other country in the world to satisfy the cosmetic beauty demands of the rich. Private hospitals receive about 60 percent of the Ministry of Health's budget, while the public hospitals receive only about 40 percent.

Two-thirds of all Brazilians are classified as poor. Of these, 71 percent do not have running water, 79 percent have no refrigeration, and 85 percent have no sewage disposal. Disease is a major problem. Every six seconds a Brazilian baby dies from a diarrhea-related disease. Leprosy, tuberculosis, and malaria are all a problem in the settler towns of Amazonia. One million

In the remoter regions of the rain forest, such as here in Rondônia state, primary health care is dispensed by traveling workers. Here a dentist tends to a Urueu Wau-Wau Indian boy.

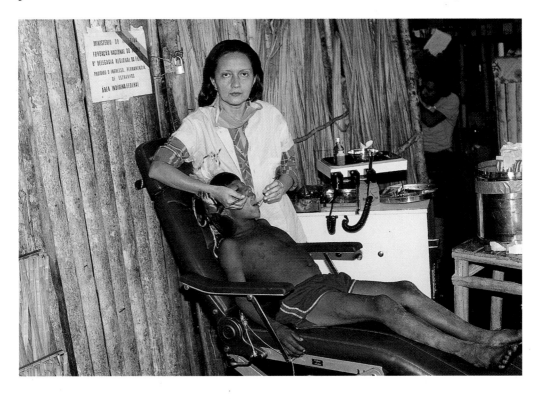

people suffer from malaria. An estimated 40 million Brazilians are malnourished. The average height of a fully grown Brazilian man is equivalent to that of an average 15-year-old boy in the United States; a Brazilian woman's is the equivalent to that of an average 12-year-old girl in the United States.

Life expectancy in Brazil largely depends on income level. The average life expectancy for women (in 1997) was 66.3 years and for men 56.78 years, but in the northeast it is ten years less because of the harshness of life there. In 1997, infant mortality stood at 53.4 deaths per 1,000 births and the size of the average Brazilian family dropped from over six children in 1940 to just over two children in 1997. The fall in Brazil's birth rate during the last part of the 20th century was one of the most dramatic in the world.

Food and Drink

Brazil has an abundance of fresh food and the diet of many Brazilians consists of their local produce. Although there are regional variations, from seafood on the coast to spicy food in the African-influenced state of Bahia, Brazilian food is usually quite similar throughout the country. Many Brazilians start their day with a *café com leite* (coffee with hot milk), made with Brazilian coffee. For breakfast they might eat fruit such as pawpaw or mango, along with freshly baked bread with cheese and meat, or perhaps a yogurt.

Once they have drunk the morning coffee, most Brazilians do not take milk in their coffee for the rest of the day. Instead, they drink a small, very strong and sweet black coffee called *cafezinho*. People say Brazilians take their coffee as strong as the devil, as hot as hell, and as sweet as love! *Cafezinho* is often drunk at stand-up bars.

Brazilians eat their main meal at lunchtime. *Almoço* (lunch) requires a healthy appetite, as Brazilian meals are very generous. They usually consist of *arroz* (rice), *feijão* (black beans), and *farofel* (manioc flour), which

HOW BRAZILIANS SPEND THEIR MONEY

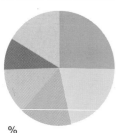

%
25.3 Food and drink

21.3 Housing and energy

15 Transportation and communication

12.9 Clothing

9.1 Health

16.4 Other

Source: Government of Brazil, 1997

Feijoada

Feijoada is the national dish of Brazil. It is a meat stew usually made from pork served with rice and a bowl of black beans. An orange slice, peppers, and manioc flour are served as accompaniments. There are many regional varieties and the meat used often depends on what the chef has in the kitchen that day. The dish was invented by slaves who had to make do with their masters' leftovers, and so put left-over bits of pig such as the hooves, tail, and ears together with black beans, which were cheap and readily available. On Saturdays, most Rio restaurants serve *feijoada completa* for lunch. It is washed down with a glass of *aguardente* (sugarcane alcohol).

is served with either *carne* (red meat), *frango* (chicken), or *peixe* (fish). The diet of modern Brazilians reflects the food of their ancestors. Native Amazonians have always used manioc (cassava) as a food staple and the African slaves lived on beans and rice. Less substantial options are available from *lanchonetes* (stand-up fast-food bars that serve sandwiches) and *suco* (juice) bars. *Suco* bars are found everywhere.

Molho de Pimenta e Limão

This spicy sauce is eaten with many dishes. Serve it in a separate bowl as an accompaniment to *feijoada completa*.

6 hot red or green jalapeños (peppers), seeded and chopped small
1 small onion, chopped small
1 clove of crushed garlic
4 fl oz of lime or lemon juice
Salt

Chop up all the ingredients very small and then put them into a blender, adding a little lime juice until you have a runny sauce.

One of the great delights of Brazil is its fruit drinks. Brazil has many exotic fruits, most of which are never seen outside the country, and Brazilians love to make juice from these fruits. One drink particularly popular with children is fresh *caldo de cana* (sugarcane juice). Another drink second only to cola in popularity is guaraná, which is made from the berry of a plant found in the Amazon. It has a sweet, bland taste.

In the rich, industrialized cities of the southeast, ownership of consumer goods is high, but in the northeast and Amazonia many live in a traditional way without modern appliances.

WHAT DO BRAZILIANS OWN?

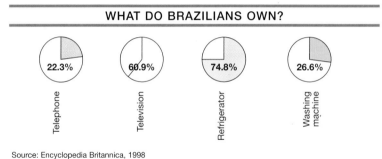

Telephone	Television	Refrigerator	Washing machine
22.3%	60.9%	74.8%	26.6%

Source: Encyclopedia Britannica, 1998

Dinner is eaten late (often not before 10:00 P.M.) in cities such as Rio and São Paulo, and consists of the same food as lunch. Because of Brazil's large immigrant population it is possible to buy excellent Japanese, Italian, and Indian food in major cities.

National Holidays and Festivals

Many of Brazil's public holidays are based on the calendar of the Roman Catholic church. In addition to the set holidays, there are four extra religious days that are selected by each municipality. Each city also celebrates the day of its founding and the day of its patron saint: Rio celebrates January 20 and São Paulo January 25. There are local festivals that reflect Brazil's mixed cultural heritage. In Salvador February 2 is a holiday to celebrate Iemanjá, the Afro-Brazilian goddess of the sea. Between June 15 and June 30, the Amazon folk festival is held in Manaus and in October, in the southern city of Blumenau, the descendants of German migrants host their own Oktoberfest, modeled on Munich's famous beer festival.

National Holidays

January 1	New Year's Day
Feb/March	Carnival: four days before Ash Wednesday
March/April	Good Friday, Easter Monday
April 21	Tiradentes Day: Discovery of Brazil
May 1	Labor Day
May/June	Corpus Christi
September 7	Independence Day
October 12	Virgin of the Conception Day: Brazil's Patron Saint
November 2	Dia dos Finados: the Day of the Dead
November 15	Proclamation of the Republic Day
December 25	Christmas Day

Sports

You do not need to look very far in Brazil to see all sorts of sports being played and watched. Old Italian immigrants may play bowls while third-generation Japanese play baseball. On the beaches of Rio people play volleyball, which is Brazil's second sport after soccer.

Pelé

Pelé is probably the most famous soccer player who ever lived. His is a rags-to-riches story. Pelé was born Édson Arantes do Nascimento on October 23, 1940, to a poor family. He first played for Brazil's national team when he was 17. The team won its first World Cup in 1958 and Pelé was still playing when Brazil won the competition in Mexico in 1970. All the statistics about Pelé are amazing. His career lasted 22 years and he scored 1,282 goals, 112 of which were for the national team. He won 53 titles, including three World Cups. After his playing career ended in Brazil, Pelé played for two seasons in the United States. When he retired, his final match took place between his then team, the New York Cosmos, and his old Brazilian team, Santos. Pelé played the first half for the New York Cosmos and the second for Santos!

Known as *O Rei* (the king) in Brazil, Pelé is greeted by presidents, kings, and queens wherever he travels in the world as Brazil's sports ambassador. In a game that sometimes is accused of being corrupt, Pelé has been a shining example of good behavior and impeccable manners.

Brazil has produced many leading Formula One (international car racing) drivers, including Emerson Fittipaldi and Nelson Piquet. The most famous and successful Brazilian Formula One driver was Ayrton Senna, whose life was tragically ended at the age of 34 when he crashed on a racetrack in 1994.

Soccer

The undisputed leader of Brazilian sports is *futebol* (soccer). Brazil is used to having the most exciting national soccer team in the world and some of the finest clubs. It became used to winning international tournaments throughout much of the 20th century. Brazil has won the World Cup a record four times: in 1958, 1962, 1970, and 1994. After its third World Cup win, Brazil was allowed to keep the original trophy. When Brazil was beaten by France in the 1998 World Cup final, the country was plunged into a week of depression.

One of soccer's great attractions is that anybody can play since the equipment needed—goalposts and a ball—is easily improvised. Children play barefoot in streets and parks and many dream of becoming good enough to escape from the poverty into which they are born. Teams are fanatically supported and each game has a carnival atmosphere. Brazil has some of the world's largest soccer stadiums: the Maracanã stadium in Rio crams in 180,000 spectators, and the Morumbi stadium in São Paulo holds 120,000. Rivalry between teams is intense and generally good-natured. Supporters create their own very rhythmic music.

So strong is the national passion for soccer in Brazil that during the World Cup many factories install televisions so that workers will not take days off to watch the matches. Many businesses simply close down during the competition.

Religion

Brazil is officially a Roman Catholic country and claims the largest Catholic population in the world. However, in recent years Protestant Evangelism has become increasingly popular. Many Brazilians are followers of an African religion such as *candomblé*, which was brought to Brazil by black African slaves.

Candomblé

Candomblé is the best known of the African religions in Brazil. Its center is Bahia, home to the largest black population. Candomblé is known by different names throughout Brazil: in Rio it is called *macumba*. In Bahia, *candomblé* practices such as washing the steps of the Bonfim church are now part of the Catholic calendar. In Rio on New Year's Eve, a million people of all religions, dressed in white, pack the beaches to throw offerings into the sea for the festival of the goddess, Iemanjá (left), so that she can protect them through the coming year.

Candomblé followers believe that everyone has an *orixá* (god) who guides and protects them. Each *orixá* has a different personality and history that determines the way their ward behaves. To discover a person's *orixá*, a priest or priestess throws seashells and then interprets what they mean according to how they land.

Brazil's diverse religious make-up has three main influences: the religion of the native people of Brazil, the Catholic and Protestant churches, and African religions.

Each of the native peoples of Brazil has its own belief system, often based around narratives associated with their ancestors. These ancestors are evoked from tree trunks or other natural places by singing or dancing, or by painting the body in symbolic colors. Some groups in the Amazon lay their villages out in a systematic way, with the huts following the trajectory of the sun.

Catholicism and African Religion

The Portuguese colonists brought Catholicism as a mission to convert the native people. Catholicism is still a major influence in Brazil's spiritual life. Saints are believed to have healing properties. The patron saint of Brazil is the Virgin of the Conception (*Nossa Senhora Aparecida*). People place wax offerings in church in thanks for recovery from an illness or accident, the offerings resemble whichever part of the body has been cured.

African slaves, forbidden by their masters from practicing their religion, found similarities between the Catholic saints and their own gods, and so adapted the African gods and worship to fit the Catholic faith. For example, when masters thought their slaves were praying to Saint George, the Catholic saint of war, the slaves were actually praying to Ogun, their own god of war. This merging of religious beliefs is known as syncretism and still underpins much of Brazil's religious life today.

The *Evangélicos*

In the last decades of the 20th century, the Catholic church lost many followers to Protestant Evangelicalism. Protestants have worshiped in Brazil since the 19th century but their numbers were small. The 1889 constitution allowed religious freedom for all, but Catholicism remained the most powerful faith. Today, it is estimated that at least 10 percent of Catholics, often poorer Brazilians, have converted to Protestant Evangelicalism. The *Evangélicos*, as they are called in Brazil, appear modern. They broadcast services and demonstrate "miracle" cures live on their own TV station and have their own newspaper. The Catholic church is sometimes seen as being out of touch with the people. Other people are turning back to the African religions for the same reason.

The city of Brasília is believed by some people to lie at the center of a magnetic field that gives off cosmic energy. As a result it has attracted a variety of modern cults, several of them associated with the end of the world.

One of Brazil's most famous cults was that of the 19th-century Catholic priest Padre Cicero. He was considered a messiah who would turn Brazil's dry *sertão* region into a lush garden of paradise. Plaster statuettes of the priest were adorned with offerings and his church became a popular shrine.

The Future

"If we wished to, we could make of this country a great nation."

Brazilian independence fighter Tiradentes

With its abundance of natural resources, Brazil is often described as a country of the future and a land of unlimited possibilities. Economically, the country is in a much better state than it has been for years and, despite recent setbacks, the reforms of the 1990s have brought much-needed stability. At the beginning of the 21st century, however, Brazil's development is somewhat short of its full potential, both economically and socially.

The reasons for this mixed picture are complex. As a whole, the Brazilian economy has recovered from the currency crises of the late 1990s. Exports are healthy and industry is expanding, particularly in the area of communications and new technology. Inflation is under control and the exchange rate of the real has become stable, creating a fertile environment for industrial growth. After the instability of 1997, foreign investors are once more looking to Brazil, with its impressive infrastructure, huge natural resources, and large workforce, as an attractive investment opportunity. Brazil's balance between imports and exports is healthier than it has been for nearly a decade.

Despite these positive economic indicators and renewed interest from abroad, many of Brazil's traditional problems remain. A major factor is the deeply embedded social inequality that permeates every aspect

The prospect of being able to supply all its electricity from hydroelectric power led Brazil to build projects such as the Itaipu Dam in the south of the country

FACT FILE

- After China, Brazil experienced the second-largest drop in birthrate in the second half of the 20th century.

- Brazil has the highest disparity of wealth in the world, with the richest 10 percent of people enjoying 50.6 percent of the nation's income.

- The poorest 50 percent and the richest 1 percent of Brazilians have a similar share of the nation's income.

- In 1995 over 50 percent of the country's 65 million children did not attend school.

- Of the 75 million Brazilians eligible to vote, 40 percent are either semi- or totally illiterate.

of Brazilian life. For the majority of Brazilians daily life is a struggle and, in order to feed themselves, they plan no further than from day to day. Their children do not go to school because any income they can earn helps provide the daily food. Unable to read themselves, the parents often do not understand that an educated child would help their situation in the long term. But if Brazil is to advance as a nation more of the country's wealth must reach the poorest members of society

Possible Solutions

Recently, there have been several grass-root movements in Brazil that have had such a positive effect on their immediate area that the rest of the country has sat up and taken notice. The most famous example comes in the southern city of Curitiba (*see* page 100). Under Mayor Jaime Lerner's radical urban planning, the residents of Curitiba have seen their standard of living rise. They enjoy a good quality of life and take pride in their city. Crucially, the gulf between the haves and have-nots is less in Curitiba than anywhere else in Brazil. Other Brazilian cities are now actively following Curitiba's lead by concentrating on improving the urban infrastructure and planning for the future.

At the end of the 20th century, Curitiba set a good example of future planning in the way Brasília had failed to do at the middle of the century. Brasília's poor quality of life for residents, its continuing gulf between the haves and have-nots, and the shab-

Political Reforms

The Cardoso government has shown considerable commitment to political reform, introducing legislation to change the way that parties are elected to Congress and thereby cutting off the prospect of, or the need for, a return to military rule. Steps have also been taken to restrict the influence that individual political parties can have on the media, limiting access to television and radio time. In addition, quotas have been introduced to increase the number of women in government, both at local and national level. Roseana Sarney, daughter of the former president, was the first woman to become a state governor in Brazil (in Maranhão state) in the mid-1990s.

biness of the *favelas* that surround the impressive center have been painful lessons for Brazil, proving that success lies not in grandiose schemes but in small-scale planning. If cities such as Curitiba point the way to Brazil's future, a strategy is urgently needed to change the social structure that has allowed such an immense gulf to appear between the rich and the poor. If Brazil would create a climate of greater social justice, experts believe a strategy for economic growth would not be far behind.

The End of the Booms

Economically the country has made huge strides since the hyperinflation of the 1980s, but the international currency crisis of 1997 proved how precarious this recovery could be. The country's wealth and industrial output is vast, but it is the distribution of the wealth and the use of profit to build an adequate infrastructure that will prove the long-term challenge in the next decades. Brazil's wealth has historically been built on a series of booms. It remains for government to continue development while reining in some of the more destructive aspects of international business that threaten to widen the gap between rich and poor and to ruin the ecology of Brazil itself.

Henrique Cardoso, first as finance minister and then from 1994 as president, has been credited with bringing Brazil's economic problems under control.

Almanac

POLITICAL

Country name:
Official long form: Federal Republic
of Brazil
Short form: Brazil
Local long form: *República Federativa
do Brasil*
Local short form: *Brasil*

Nationality:
noun: Brazilian (s)
adjective: Brazilian

Official language: Portuguese

Capital city: Brasília

Type of government: federal republic

Suffrage (voting rights): everyone 16
years and over

National anthem: "The Peaceful
Banks of the Ipiranga"

National holiday: September 7
(Independence Day)

Flag:

GEOGRAPHICAL

Location: South America;
latitudes 10 00° south
and longitudes 55 00° west

Climate: Tropical in north
temperate in south

Total area: 3,284,426 square miles
(8,506,663 sq. km)
land: 93.5%
water: 6.5%

Coastline: 4,654 miles (7,491 km)

Terrain: lowlands in north,
uplands in center,
narrow coastal strip.

Highest point: Pico da Bandeira,
9,495 feet (2,894 m)
Lowest point: no areas below
sea level

Natural resources: gold, iron ore,
manganese, nickel, phospates,
platinum, tin, uranium,
petroleum, hydroelectric
power, timber

Land use (1993 est.):
arable land: 5%

forests and woodland: 58%
permanent pastures: 22%
permanent crops: 1%
other: 14%

Literacy:
total population: 83.3%
male: 83.3%
female: 83.2%

POPULATION

Population: 171.8 million (1999 est.)

Population density: 51 people per square mile (20 per sq. km)

Population growth rate (1999 est.): 01.16%

Birthrate (1999 est.): 20.42 births per 1,000 of the population

Death rate (1999 est.): 8.79 deaths per 1,000 of the population

Sex ratio (1999 est.): 97 males per 100 females

Total fertility rate (1999 est.): 2.28 children born per woman

Infant mortality rate (1999 est.): 35.37 deaths per 1,000 live births

Life expectancy at birth (1999 est.):
total population: 64.06 years
male: 59.35 years
female: 69.01 years

ECONOMY

Currency: real (R$); 1 R$= 100 centavos

Exchange rate (1999): $1 = 1.501 R$

Gross national product (1999): $784 billion (eighth-largest economy in the world)

Average annual growth rate (1990–1997): 3.4%

GNP per capita (1999 est.): $4,790

Average annual inflation rate (1985–1996): 12.1%

Unemployment rate (1998 est.): 8.5%

Exports (1997): $53 billion
Imports (1997): $61.4 billion

Foreign aid received (1996): $487 million

Human Development Index
(an index scaled from 0 to 100 combining statistics indicating adult literacy, years of schooling, life expectancy, and income levels):
80.9 (U.S. 94.2)

TIME LINE—BRAZIL

World History

Brazilian History

c. 50,000 B.C.

c. **40,000** Modern humans—*Homo sapiens sapiens*—emerge.

c. **20,000 B.C.** Hunter-gatherers cross the land bridge between Asia and North America.

c. 10,000 B.C.

c. **A.D. 1** Birth of Christ.

306 Emperor Constantine promotes Christianity throughout the Roman empire.

c. 1000 Vikings reach American continent but do not settle.

c. **10,000 B.C.** First permanent human settlements in Brazil.

c. **200 B.C.** Human settlement throughout Brazil.

c. **A.D. 400–700.** Complex village society at Marajó Island in northern Amazonia.

A.D. 1500

c. 1350–1550 Italian Renaissance leads to rebirth of the arts and classical learning in Europe.

1500 Pedro Alvares Cabral lands in Brazil.

1530 Portuguese set up royal colony at São Vicente.

1650–1700 Explosion of observational science in Europe leads to the new physics, discovery of microscopic life and blood circulation, and the invention of the steam engine.

1545–63 Council of Trent leads to Catholic church's counterattack against Luther in the Counter Reformation.

1517 Martin Luther begins Protestant Reformation.

1695 Gold discovered in Minas Gerais.

1640s–1650s *Bandeirantes* penetrate South American interior as far as Peruvian Andes.

1620s–1654 Dutch forces control much of north-eastern Brazil.

1600

1567 French ousted from Guanabara Bay and city of Rio de Janeiro founded.

1550s Sugarcane planted in northeastern Brazil. First slaves transported from Africa.

1549 Tomé de Souza becomes first governor of Brazil. First capital established at Salvador in Bahia.

1700

c. 1750 Industrial Revolution begins in England.

1776 American Declaration of Independence.

1789 French Revolution begins.

1799 Napoleon Bonaparte becomes emperor of France.

1752 Treaty of Madrid divides up territory of Guarani missions between Portugal and Spain.

1760 Jesuits expelled from Brazil.

1763 Capital transfers from Salvador to Rio.

1789 Conspiracy discovered at Ouro Prêto to overthrow Portuguese rule.

1997 World currency crisis sparked by Southeast Asian economic collapse.

1989 Collapse of communism in Eastern Europe.

1963–1975 The Vietnam War.

2000

1994 Cardoso launches Real Plan.

1992 Rio Summit focuses world attention on the plight of Amazon rain forest.

1964–1985 Period of military rule.

1960 Capital moves to Brasília.

1960

1800

1807 Napoleon invades Portugal. Portuguese court flees to Rio.

1815 Napoleon defeated at Waterloo.

1810–1824 Spanish colonies in mainland South America win independence.

1820s Beginning of Brazilian coffee boom.

1822 Brazilian independence declared.

1840 Dom Pedro II declared emperor of Brazil at age of fourteen.

1888 Slavery abolished.

1889 Military coup leads to declaration of Brazilian republic.

1945 End of World War II, defeat of Germany.

1939 World War II begins.

1929 Wall Street Crash, beginning of Great Depression.

1918 World War I ends.

1917 Revolution in Russia leads to establishment of Soviet Union.

1914 World War I begins.

1950–1954 Second Vargas term leads to rapid industrialization.

1942 Brazil enters World War II.

1930 Gétulio Vargas becomes president and begins transformation of Brazil.

1917 After repeated German attacks on Brazilian boats, Brazil enters World War I.

1890–1910 Brazilian rubber boom.

1900

Glossary

Abbreviation:
Port.=Portuguese

aguardente (**Port.**): Strong, alcoholic drink made from sugarcane.

abertura (**Port.**): Literally "the opening-up." Refers to the gradual movement from military to civilian government in Brazil in the early 1980s.

baroque: An elaborate style of art and architecture originating in Italy during the 16th century and relying for its effects on dramatic contrast and ornamentation.

bandeirantes (**Port.**): Men from São Paulo who explored Brazil's interior in the 17th and 18th centuries looking for gold and native people to enslave.

bossa nova: Music that mixes North American jazz with Brazilian influences.

caboclo (**Port.**): Native of the Amazon, usually of mixed European and native ancestry.

caiman: A type of large reptile similar to a crocodile and native to Brazil.

candomblé (**Port.**): Afro-Brazilian religion originating in the region of Bahia.

carioca (**Port.**): Native of Rio de Janeiro.

Carnival: Four-day fiesta to celebrate the start of Lent, involving large-scale processions that include elaborate floats and costumes.

cerrado (**Port.**): Very fertile savannah.

coup: A sudden overthrow of the government by a small group, often military in nature.

cruzeiro: Former national currency of Brazil.

escolas de samba (**Port.**): Large samba clubs that take part in the Rio Carnival.

Estado Novo (**Port.** "the new state"): Period from 1930 to 1945 under President Getúlio Vargas involving large-scale industrialization and social changes in Brazil.

exports: Goods sold by one country to another.

favela (**Port.**): Slum or shanty town.

favelado (**Port.**): Slum-dweller.

feijoada (**Port.**): Brazil's national dish, a stew made out of meat with black beans, served with rice.

futvolei (**Port.**): Volleyball played with the feet.

gaiola (**Port.**): Riverboat used for travel on the Amazon.

garimpeiro (**Port.**): Prospector or miner. The original name for illegal diamond prospectors.

gaúcho (**Port.**): A cowboy in southern Brazil or anyone from the state of Rio Grande do Sul in southern Brazil.

guaraná (**Port.**): Amazonian shrub whose berry is believed to have magical powers. Also a popular soft drink.

hyperinflation: A rapid increase in prices.

imports: Goods bought by one country from another.

industrialization: The movement of an economy from producing raw materials to the production of manufactured or processed goods.

interest rates: The standard rate at which interest is charged on loans in a country. Rates are often raised by the government to moderate economic expansion and lowered to boost it.

lanchonete (**Port.**): Snack bar.

meninos de rua (**Port.** "street kids"): Brazilian children who have no parents or place to live.

MERCOSUL: Portuguese name for trading bloc of South American countries, offering each other preferential trading conditions.

mestiço (**Port.**): Person of mixed Indian and European parentage.

mulatto: Person of mixed black and European parentage.

Orixá: A candomblé god.

pampas: Grassy South American plain.

Pantanal: Large, alluvial flood plain in southwest Brazil.

paulistano (**Port.**): Native of the city of São Paulo.

planalto (**Port.**): Wide area of elevated land.

quilombo (**Port.**): Community of ex-slaves in 17th-century Brazil.

real: Brazil's national currency from 1994.

rodoviária (**Port.**): Bus station.

samba: The most popular Brazilian music, African in origin.

sertão (**Port.**): Arid area in northeastern Brazil.

suco (**Port.**): Fruit juice.

telenovelas (**Port.**): Popular TV dramas that air most nights of the week.

terra firme (**Port.**): "solid ground." The area where most people live in the Amazon region.

trade winds: Winds from the north and south Atlantic Ocean that bring weather systems in to Southern America.

tributary: Smaller river that flows into a larger river that has an oulet on the ocean.

tropicalismo (**Port.**): Cultural movement, mixing the influence of several races, originating in Bahia in the late 1960s.

várzea (**Port.**): Very fertile flood plain of tropical river such as the Amazon.

Bibliography

Major Sources Used for This Book

Box, Ben. *Brazil Handbook*. London: Footprint, 1998.

Marshall, Andrew. *Brazil*. London: Thames and Hudson, 1966.

Rocha, Jan. *Brazil–A Guide to the People, Politics and Culture*. London: LAB, 1997.

Rodman, Selden. *The Brazil Traveler*. Devin–Adair, 1975.

South America, Central America, and the Caribbean Statistical Survey–7th edition. London: Europa Publishing, Ltd, 1999.

CIA World Factbook (www.odci.gov/cia/publications/ factbook)

Economist World in Figures 2000 London: Economist Books, 2000

General Further Reading

Encyclopedia of World Cultures ed. Lynda A. Bennett. Boston: G.K. Hall & Co., 1992.

World Reference Atlas. London: Dorling Kindersley, 2000.

The Kingfisher History Encyclopedia. New York: Kingfisher, 1999.

Student Atlas. New York: Dorling Kindersley, 1998.

The World Book Encyclopedia. Chicago: Scott Fetzer Company, 1999.

Further Reading About Brazil

Page, Joseph, A. *The Brazilians*. Addison–Wesley, 1995.

Pendel, George. *A History of Latin America*. New York: Penguin, 1973.

Selby, Nick, et al. *Brazil*. London: APA Publications, 1999.

Williamson, Edwin. *The Penguin History of Latin America*. New York: Penguin, 1992

Some Websites About Brazil

www.brasilemb.org (site of the Brazilian Embassy in Washington, D.C.)

www.brasil-brazil.co.br (information on Brazilian history, culture, and economy)

Index

Acknowledgments

Cover Photo Credits
Embratur/Brazilian Tourist Board: (Blue parrot); **Trip:** Mike Mirecki (Sugar Loaf Mountain overview); D. Harding (Rio Carnival)

Photo Credits
AKG London: 50, 55, 56, 60, 63; **Corbis:** Paul Almasy 34; Achivio Iconografico, SA 53; Bettermann 68; Jeremy Cook 112; James Davies/Eye Ubiquitous 43; David G. Houser 64, 86; Wolfgang Kaehler 29; OLArry Lee 36; Stephanie Maze 42, 46, 82, 89, 101, 104, 114; Reuters Inc 94; Julia Waterlow 116; Peter Wilson 44, 59 **Embratur/Brazilian Tourist Board:** 30, 38, 91; **Hulton:** 67; **Hutchison Library:** 79, 84, 88, 107, Richard Howe 16, Edward Parker 17; **Popperfoto:** 70, Reuters Inc. 119; **Still Pictures:** Julio Etchart **South American Pictures:** Jason P. Howe 95, 109; Marion Morrison 102; Tony Morrison 6, 19, 21, 24, 28, 76, 92; **Tony Stone** 40; Thierry Cazabon 32; Jacques Jangoux 20; Will and Demi McIntyre 18, 12; **Trip:** P. Kerry 37; Mike Mirecki 31; P. Musson 23, 99; **Werner Forman Archive** 48